Swans of Other Worlds
Kazimir Malevich and the
Origins of Abstraction
in Russia

Studies in the Fine Arts:
The Avant-Garde, No. 2

Stephen C. Foster, Series Editor
Associate Professor of Art History
University of Iowa

Other Titles in This Series

Swans of Other Worlds

Kazimir Malevich and the
Origins of Abstraction
in Russia

by
Charlotte Douglas

umi
RESEARCH PRESS

Produced and distributed by
UMI Research Press
an imprint of
University Microfilms International
Ann Arbor, Michigan 48106

Library of Congress Cataloging in Publication Data

Douglas, Charlotte Cummings, 1936-
Swans of other worlds.

(Studies in the fine arts : The avant-garde ; 2)
Bibliography: p.
Includes index.
1. Malevich, Kazimir Severinovich, 1878-1935.
2. Suprematism in art. 3. Avant-garde (Aesthetics)—
Russia. I. Title. II. Series: Studies in the fine arts :
Avant-garde ; 2.

N6999.M34D68   759.7   80-13165
ISBN 0-8357-1058-0

For Alan, Jamie, Neva and Shandy.

Contents

List of Illustrations

Acknowledgments

This book was written with the assistance of many people and institutions. I find it especially difficult to express adequately my gratitude to John E. Bowlt and the Institute of Modern Russian Culture at Blue Lagoon, Texas. Without the repeated and cheerful help of Professor Bowlt and the resources of the Institute which he directs, much of the basic work for this study would have been logistically impossible.

Research in the Soviet Union during 1975 and 1976 was conducted with the crucial, sustained support of the International Research and Exchanges Board and their admirably competent staff: Allen Kassof, Daniel Matuszewski and Carolyn Rogers. I thank them well and warmly.

In the USSR my work was facilitated by the generous cooperation of the Ministry of Higher Education, the Ministry of Culture of the USSR, the State Tretiakov Gallery, Moscow, and the State Russian Museum, Leningrad. I owe a special debt for guidance and assistance to A. Khalturin of the Ministry of Culture, to V. Pushkariev, and to the History Faculty of Moscow State University, especially Dmitrii Sarabianov, my supervisor. I consulted the holdings of several Soviet archives; in particular I would like to acknowledge the help of the staffs of the Central State Archives for Literature and Art and the Archival Section of the Russian Museum. Many of my Soviet colleagues contributed their time and knowledge unsparingly; special mention should be made of long and informative discussions with Nikolai Khardzhiev, Evgenii Kovtun, Anna Leporskaia, Alla Povelikhina and Vasilii Rakitin.

The staff of the Stedelijk Museum, Amsterdam, the holder of the largest collection of Malevich's work in the West, was consistently prompt in responding to numerous inquiries. In the United States the collections of the Widener and Fogg Libraries of Harvard University and the New York Public Library were particularly useful. This volume derives from my doctoral dissertation written at The University of Texas at Austin. For their encouragement during this period I offer my sincere thanks to Donald Goodall of the Department of Art and Sidney Monas of the Department of Slavic Languages. I am grateful also to Jo Ann Hawkins of the Interlibrary Loan Service of The University of Texas Library. For several years she was indefatigable in her search for the rare bibliographical material fundamental to this work.

Portions of this book have appeared earlier in *The Art Journal, Russian*

Literature Triquarterly, *Russian Review* and *Art in America*. They are used here by permission.

Charlotte Douglas
May, 1980

Introduction

Kazimir Malevich's "Supreme" abstractions seem to have burst upon Russia's artistic scene from nowhere. At "0-10. The Last Futurist Exhibition" held in Petrograd in December 1915, Malevich showed thirty-nine completely abstract canvases, including his famous black "Square."[1] Not one had appeared before. Although this single body of work has had a direct and persistent visual impact on Western art—at first in Russia in the objectless creations of the early Soviet period and then throughout the Bauhaus school of international modernism—very little is known about the origin of Suprematism.[2] For American art the missing links are felt especially keenly: Suprematism is an important ancestor of the "post-painterly" (Greenberg) alternative to Abstract Expressionism. The precise historical and theoretical relationship of Suprematism to American art of the 1950's and 60's—the "Systemic" (Alloway), "ABC" (Rose) or "Minimal" art of such painters as Elsworth Kelly, Al Held, Ad Reinhardt, Alexander Liberman (b. Kiev), and Barnett Newman—is still not clear. There is no question, however, about the visual similarity, the large well-defined forms and intense color, to the work of Malevich, nor about the fact that it was Malevich who first established the whole context in which American artists have found significant and esthetically rewarding problems.[3]

The results of this study tend to complicate the generally assumed direct descent of Suprematism from Cubism (an assumption too simply made by analogy with Leger) and thus set up an interesting parallel with the course of American art. It is now axiomatic that the rational art of the past twenty years evolved as an extension of Abstract Expressionism; Suprematism's straightforward evolution from Cubism thus presented a seemingly different case, and comparisons with early geometricism were difficult to make without accounting for the anomalous development. The implications of this study are significant, for they say that in no demonstrable case did Cubism alone lead to a lasting abstraction. Apparently, contemporary artists did not so much "rediscover" Malevich as "re-live" the course from Expressionism (and in Malevich's case, Futurism, described by a contemporary as "emotional impressionism") to Suprematism, this time with the benefit of Malevich's first definitions. American artists have pursued to radical solutions many questions merely raised by Malevich and now find themselves far beyond his early geometry; but their work in turn serves as dramatic validation of Malevich's original insights. The 1915 "Zero-Ten" exhibi-

tion now appears incredibly prophetic. In addition to the abstract counter-
reliefs shown by Tatlin, several pieces of sculpture were exhibited which might
be viewed as "found" or "ready-made" or "pop," and Suprematism not only
pointed to geometry and minimalism, but also to conceptual art.[4] Most im-
pressively, in many of these early works Malevich managed that great feat of
American minimalists: an existential simultaneity, the stable hovering above
art as signification and art as object.

Looking back to the first half of our century for the beginnings of Suprematism and for our own abstract beginnings, one finds a veritable soup of
esthetic notions and stylistic innovations on the boil throughout Europe; but in
Russia, paradoxically, a country on the very edge of Europe, isolated geographi-
cally and linguistically, were amassed the most complete and international
exhibitions and examples of the new art. Here were absorbed, out of chrono-
logical order and context, the widest range of new artistic ideas anywhere in
the world. Among the avant-garde, interest in the new art was cosmopolitan,
avid, and disinterested as to nationality; and this circumstance has contributed to, if not actually caused, persistent questions about the originality
of the early Russian contribution to the modern movement, especially about
that of Malevich. For, in some sense, the new Russian art resembled *all* of the
new art, and in later years this has raised the awkward question of "influences."
That Malevich could have made such an uncompromising and fertile visual
statement in 1915 without a great deal of help from work which was moving
in the same direction is, of course, unthinkable; but significant progress toward
the understanding of the actual evolution of Suprematism has been hampered
by many things. The whole modern movement in Russia has been a source of
embarrassment for the Soviet government and, until recently, it has preferred
to keep scholarly research to a minimum. Even the works themselves were
(and for the most part are still) kept "in reserve," i.e. out of view, at museums
and galleries. By comparison, the course of modernism in Western Europe has
been enthusiastically explored, and temptation has been great to merely ascribe
the Russian work to Western "borrowings." Those not in agreement with this
version of art history were apt to take up the diametrically oppposed stand, and
claim that Russia had been "isolated" at the time and had developed modern
forms without any awareness at all of the course of art in Europe. This view
was often fostered by the artists themselves, as they tried to defend the originality of their work. Retrospective personal and nationalistic competition has
been fierce, and has in several cases led painters and writers to date their works
more in accordance with "emotional" than "factual" truth. The commercializa-
tion of early Russian modern art certainly has not helped in this matter.

Actually, the situation seems to have been a more balanced one in which
original and important Russian innovations can be recognized, while taking into
account the avant-garde's thorough knowledge of all of the new art. It is easy

enough to point to motifs and details in Malevich's work which demonstrate his awareness of Van Gogh, Leger, and Picasso. It would have been strange if he had not known this work, and Malevich never made any attempt to disguise the sources of his stylistic experiments. The strongest intellectual influences seem to have come through the ideas of Kulbin, Kandinsky, Matiushin, Kruchenykh and Bergson, from Worringer, Helmholtz, Denis, Fechner, Wundt and Lipps; in other words, from Expressionism. Malevich's ready use of P.D. Uspensky's formal vocabulary derives from this orientation;[5] and for the same reason he found the esthetics of both Boccioni and the Puteaux Cubists congenial. Although the Futurist and Cubist idioms were instrumental to Malevich's search for essential form, he ultimately found them too dependent on visual reality to express his views of an invisible one. In the final analysis, of course, Malevich's selection and combination of these elements, and their "crossing over" into Suprematism—an event which Donald Judd has called "mysterious, incredible and awesome"—was the product of a traditionally Russian philosophical orientation and his own personal genius.

The dating of Malevich's work has for a number of years been a matter of controversy. In *The Objectless World,* published as volume 11 of the Bauhaus Books in 1927 (first translated into English from the German as *The Non-Objective World* in 1959)[6] Malevich states that Suprematism originated in 1913 and that 1914 was "the year when the square appeared." Since the Suprematist paintings were not exhibited until December 1915, however, and there are apparently no eyewitnesses to the 1914 date, it was sometimes suspected that Malevich was attempting to establish precedence over, or contemporaneity with, Leger's 1913 studies of volumes. Chapter 3 of this study makes a detailed examination of Malevich's 1913 designs for the opera, *Victory Over the Sun,* and concludes that probably the root idea for the Suprematist style came from this production. Quite recently, portions of Malevich's correspondence with Matiushin during 1914 and 1915 have been published, and these seem to indicate that Malevich actually started painting Suprematist works as such by May of 1915 when he began to re-work the decor for *Victory*. His letters show that it was in fact the backdrop curtain for the "Sun" (see Chapters 3 and 5), meant to signify victory, that was the key to his black *Square* and to the name of the new style, "Suprematism." Thus the statement made in *The Objectless World* appears to have been essentially accurate. Malevich was deliberately misleading about the dates of other work, however, and for that reason the chronology of all his paintings must be approached with caution. The dates ascribed to works mentioned in this discussion are based upon examination of all available information: catalogues, reviews, photographs, and internal evidence provided by the paintings themselves. For the most part they agree with Troels Andersen's catalogue for the Stedelijk Museum.[7]

Malevich's mysticism has been much remarked, but it appears from this study that up until 1915 such spiritual or mystical inclinations as Malevich had were no more pronounced than those of the whole Russian avant-garde, including Matiushin, Kulbin, Burliuk, and Kandinsky. Modern Russian painters were deeply aware of their legacy of seven hundred years of icon painting, and their understanding of the role of the artist in society and the nature of his work was in part an extension of this cultural experience. Unlike such early abstractionists as Kupka, Mondrian, Churlionis, and Kandinsky, Malevich did not bolster the rejection of naturalism with colorist or formal spiritualist "systems" or with musical analogies. In this respect he seems to have been unusually ahead of his time.

The documents considered in this study attest strikingly to the misunderstanding, the total absence of comprehension, the ridicule, of the new art by journalists and critics whose business it was to understand and explain. The fact is that the avant-garde lived and worked in a time that existed only in potential, that for them would never come. Such a sorry critical situation now presents problems for the historian, too. The disjunction between the art and even the most informed interpreters removes the recent past to prehistory, and those seeking the roots of their own art are obliged to become archeologists more than anything else. In his *Modern Art Exhibitions* Donald Gordon points out this problem:

> Standing without warning at the exact interface with the future, the critic (and thus his public) [could] only leaven ignorance with attempts at ridicule. Willing or not, to avoid such ignorance and guesswork in the future, the art critic must [now] perforce turn for any kind of enlightenment to—the artist himself! The ridiculed painter, his "angular fragments of painted surface," his "nursery effort" thus become the only sources of knowledge about the new art.[8]

In its discussion of the origin of Suprematism, this study attempts to attend both to the "ridiculed painter" and to his "nursery efforts," to provide something of a narrative account of the lives and work of Malevich and his friends during this period, while giving "archaeological" detail and analyses of key works and ideas. A strong effort has been made throughout to relate what was taking place in Russia to the course of the new art in Western Europe, and to the lines of communication between East and West. Perhaps this study will do something toward strengthening such communication again.

1

Post-Impressionism in Russia: 1908-1912

"An Exhibition of Modern Trends" opened on 25 April 1908 in St. Petersburg. At the *vernissage* the "Passage" on the Nevsky Prospect was packed with Petersburg journalists and critics (mostly unfriendly) and the painters and their friends, including some of the more established members of the Russian art world. On the walls of the gallery alongside pictures by the Academician Nikolai Petrovich Bogdanov-Belsky,[1] and the Petersburg contingent of the "Union of Russian Artists," Bakst, Benois and Bilibin, hung work by Russia's "artistic youth," Nikolai Kulbin, Ludmilla, David and Vladimir Burliuk, Alexandra Exter, and Aristarkh Lentulov. In the disorderly crowd Vasilii Kamensky, a fledgling poet and the editor by default of the short lived literary almanac, *Vesna*,[2] reports seeing many of the young Russian modernists: Yakulov, Malevich, Larionov, Goncharova, Filonov, Spandikov, and Tatlin.[3] Uncertain, but still feeling superior, the Petersburg intellectuals resorted to irony. Critic and writer Kornei Chukovsky:

> "Brilliant! Heavenly! A naked green woman with a violet belly button. Who is she? From what primitive islands? Can I get an introduction?"

Elegant, correctly attired N.N. Breshko-Breshkovsky from the leading Petersburg daily newspaper *The Exchange Gazette (Birzhovye Vedomosti)*:

> "But why is she green? Couldn't she just as well have been violet, and her belly button green?"
> "Oh, but she's drowned!"

Chukovsky smirked triumphantly.[4]

Not everyone was so impressed with the colors of the paintings. The correspondent for the lavish art periodical *The Golden Fleece* hardly seems to have seen the paintings, he was so disturbed by the environment. "The disorderly and slovenly arrangement of the room reminded one more of some kind of dirty barn, or of the Academy of Arts museum, than of an exhibition hall for 'modern' trends," he wrote.[5]

At one end of the room, Kulbin, ever the professor, gold glasses in place, gravely instructed the audience:

> We are impressionists, on the canvas we give our impression, i.e. our 'impressio.' We see just this way and our impression is reflected in the picture without regard for other people's banal notions about the color of the body. In the world every-

thing is relative. Even the sun is seen by some people as gold, by others as silver, others as rose, and still others as colorless. The right of the artist is to see it as it seems to him, that is his absolute right.[6]

The speaker, Nikolai Kulbin, was a doctor, with inclinations to psychiatry, and a professor at the Military Medical Academy in Petersburg. Born in 1868,[7] by the time he had reached his mid-thirties he had achieved a measure of respectability, a solidly respectable suite of offices, and an editorship of the Medical Department's contribution to the prestigious commemorative history (1802-1902) published by the War Ministry.[8] He had risen steadily in the ranks to the level of State Councilor, and so strolled about in a gold-braided general's uniform.[9] Who would have guessed that such an obviously substantial person was the "crazy doctor" now coming to the defense of the "hooligans" of the new art. In fact, this exhibition was mostly Kulbin's. He was an organizer, backer, exhibitor, as well as the chief theoretician for his group, which he called "△ — The Art Psychological Group."[10] He had a strange but convincing and vaguely familiar explanation for his devotion to the new art. With an odd smile and a far away look he would recount its beginning:

> I was walking across a bridge; I wanted to stretch my legs, I was thinking about things—about my patients—about my lectures . . . I remember my galoshes were new and still squeeked a lot. I was not at all disturbed, not in any special mood. And just at Troitskaya Square, there was a horse on its side, and a cart driver was lashing it to make it get up. I can see it all—all. And it couldn't get up; it only jerked. And at that moment the lamps all along the street flared up. It is not yet completely dark and suddenly the lamps come up. You know how pretty that is . . . That's all. Nothing more. At that moment something inside of me turned over. Just as though I had been completely dead and was saved by a miracle. I stood still, for some reason I took off my hat. You old fool, I thought, why have you killed fifty years of your life? A policeman ran up to me, "Your excellency, your excellency." He put me in a cab.[11]

"An Exhibition of Modern Trends" was the first major enterprise of Kulbin's new life, a life which would last just nine more years. He had been an amateur painter for a year or more, and just recently he had begun to lecture about town on his favorite topic, "Free Art as the Basis of Life."[12] This exhibition had been planned for months.[13] Assigned by the publisher to review the show for *Spring (Vesna),* the young writer from Perm,[14] Vasilii Kamensky, followed the senior journalist Breshko-Breshkovsky through the pushing and jostling crowd to the other end of the "Passage" where David and Vladimir Burliuk were also haranguing the crowd about the hopelessly bourgeois tastes of Petersburg journalists and extolling the new art.

A mutual friend, the painter Aristarkh Lentulov, had introduced David and his brother to Kulbin on their first visit to Petersburg some four months previously.[15] Kulbin had received them openly, invited them to take part in "Modern Trends," and introduced them to some of Petersburg's more substantial society. Kulbin's rank and profession put him in a financial and social position not enjoyed by most of the young artists, and from 1908 they took full advantage of his hospitality. In his comfortable apartment next to the Winter Palace they camped in the waiting room, helped themselves to the telephone, consulted the doctor about their illnesses and sold him their paintings. (He was clever enough to pay for paintings on the installment plan so the money would last as long as possible.) Kulbin's wife, the buxom but attractive Raisa Pavlovna, protested about the ever-present "guests," but to no avail, and she and their three children had to learn to live with the continuous activity.

Many of the painters who exhibited at "Modern Trends" were already familiar to Russian audiences. The St. Petersburg representatives of the "Union of Russian Artists" such as Bakst and Benois were former "World of Art" members and their work had been shown in Petersburg for ten years or more. David Burliuk had appeared in a large "Union of Russian Artists" exhibition more than a year previously (Dec. 1906-Jan. 1907) and in the recent (Dec. 1907-Jan. 1908) "Wreath-Stephanos" exhibition. In fact, so many Burliuks—David, Vladimir, Ludmilla—had been shown in the "Wreath," *The Golden Fleece* complained that it was "jammed full and clogged up" with the Burliuks' work.[16]

At the opening of "Modern Trends" Kamensky introduced himself to the Burliuks and Kulbin, and later he brought Viktor Khlebnikov, a fellow poet and new found friend, to meet the Burliuks. Khlebnikov had recently arrived in Petersburg from Kazan and in the fall would continue his study of mathematics at St. Petersburg University. Meanwhile he had approached Kamensky with poems for publication in *Spring*.[17] The young peoples' delight in finding one another, and their shared interest in new approaches to writing and painting, soon evolved into plans for a new "group" and publication. Until the discovery of Vladimir Mayakovsky four years later, Khlebnikov would be the principal literary *raison d'être* for the "artistic youth." Kamensky, finding himself now among painters, began himself to paint, and worked in Burliuk's studio.[18]

Two particular interests can be detected among the works shown by the "youth" at this early exhibition: the depiction of psychological states or "moods" in works called *Sadness, Boredom* and *Thoughts;* and "Post-Impressionist" landscapes such as *Lilacs and House,* and *Wharf in Yalta.* Both concerns derived from an intense interest in what might best be called 'progressive symbolism,' which involved the attempt to make effective artistic use of psychological and physiological information, as the Neo-Impressionists had done with physically based color theories. Russia was well prepared for such concepts by its advanced school of literary Symbolism which had very early looked to science as well as to mysticism for its theoretical formulations. Kulbin began to lecture on his theory of "free art" in 1908. He advanced as a fundamental premise a pan-psychic view of the world, advocated "dissonance" in art for its affective value, and elaborated a theory of "close combinations" of colors or musical tones which would affect the perceiver subliminally. Kulbin would expand and elaborate upon this theory until his death in 1917.

In the spring of 1909 Kulbin undertook his most ambitious project to date—a large exhibition—large enough to rival the "Union" or "Wreath" or "Salon" exhibitions in impact under the general title "The Impressionists." Although the Burliuks may have participated in the preparation of this show,[19] they did not exhibit any work in it, presumably because they had had their own small exhibition, "Wreath-Stephanos," with Lentulov and three other painters immediately before the opening of "The Impressionists."[20] There may also have been the feeling at the time that Kulbin and Burliuk led distinctly different trends or approaches to art, with distinctly separate followers, and that it would have been inappropriate to include them all under the title "Impressionists." Only one exhibitor in "Wreath-Stephanos," L. Baranov,[21] appeared also in Kulbin's exhibition. Kamensky, whose new work was intended originally to be shown in Burliuk's exhibition,[22] submitted his painting *(Little Birches)* instead to Kulbin.[23] Alexei Kruchenykh, a graphic artist from Kherson Province and an acquaintance of Burliuk, contributed one work *(Summer)* to "The Impressionists." Kruchenykh, who had an instructor's diploma from the Odessa Art School, had moved to Moscow in 1907. At the time of the exhibition he was achieving a reputation of sorts with his caricatures for satirical journals of Kherson dignitaries and Moscow professors.[24]

It was in the course of preparing for Kulbin's new exhibition that two of the major participants in the new art movement, Elena Guro and her husband Mikhail Matiushin, were introduced first to Kamensky and the Burliuks.[25] Matiushin in 1909 was a violinist in the St. Petersburg Court Orchestra. He had received his musical education at the Moscow Conservatory of Music,[26] and after establishing his professional career, he had begun to study painting in the Petersburg studio of Jan Tsionglinskii. There he met poet and painter, Elena Guro.[27] Guro in 1904 had illustrated a Kharkov edition of George Sand's *Grandmother Tales,* and published short stories in 1905 and 1906.[28] By the time they met Kulbin in early 1909, Matiushin and Guro had been painting in Petersburg studios for several years. Matiushin helped organize "The Impressionists" and contributed three *Landscape Studies* to it; Guro showed five drawings from her book, *Hurdy-Gurdy (Sharmanka),* which had appeared three months previously.[29]

The Russian understanding of "modernism" and the use of the term "impressionism" at this time, must be made very clear. *The Golden Fleece,* a popular sponsor of Symbolist, Post-Impressionist and Fauvist ideas in art, in their "Salon" exhibitions in 1908 and 1909 had presented Gauguin, Van Gogh, Bonnard, Serusier and Denis to the Russian public. In the fall of 1908 Genrikh Tasteven, an editor of the journal and Umberto Marinetti's future host in Russia (Marinetti remembered his "little red Russian eyes") published an article dismissing Impressionism and Neo-Impressionism as the analogue in art of realism in literature, and applauding Van Gogh, Denis, Bonnard and others for their "striving toward the new 'symbolism'."[30] *The Golden Fleece* also published Matisse's "Notes d'un peintre." Denis's essay "De Gauguin et de Van Gogh au Classicisme" appeared in two issues of the journal in 1909 and seems to have made a strong impression on the fledgling avant-garde; for the next several years traces of this essay can be found in many of their theoretical statements.[31] Yet perhaps because of the literary or decadent associations, the term 'symbolist' or even 'expressionist' never entered the vanguard vocabulary; "Impressionism" continued to be used as before, but with newly acquired Post-Impressionist implications. In the new understanding there was strong emphasis on the personal vision, the "I" of the artist. The work as an equivalent of sensation, as the reproduction of emotional and spiritual states through plastic equivalents, subjective deformation, and the primacy of the creative process in the search for meaning, were all concepts which were discussed in 1908 and 1909 and which were to enter quite directly and naturally into the ideas of the Russian Futurists. When Kulbin called his new exhibition "The Impressionists," it was the more radical definition of the term that he had in mind.

Kulbin's efforts at this time were not only directed toward the organization of exhibitions. His first publication on art appeared at the beginning of 1909[32] and during the year he lectured on his theory of free art. At the beginning of 1910 a seven page booklet, *Free Music, The Application of the New Theory of Artistic Creation to Music,* appeared (in editions of a few hundreds) in Russian, German and French.[33] At that time Kulbin was also preparing a much more ambitious literary project, *The Impressionists' Studio,* an expensive publication containing graphics and color illustrations by several of the "Impressionist" exhibitors, and prose and poetry by his friends the Burliuks and Khlebnikov.[34] *The Impressionists' Studio* was indeed a substantial exemplification of the new art. This one publication presented: Khlebnikov's famous linguistic innovations in the poem "Incantation by Laughter"; two long and seminal essays by Kulbin, "Free Art as the Basis of Life" and "Free Music"; and Nikolai Evreinov's remarkable monodrama, "A Portrayal of Love," accompanied by Evreinov's explanatory "Introduction to Monodrama" and reproductions in color of Kulbin's illustrations to the text.

The illustrative material as a whole clearly has a tendency to the "prettiness" currently in fashion and shown, for example, by *The Golden Fleece.* The elaborate decorativeness and the combination of pointillism and the curved fantastic line bear witness to the influence of folk art and art nouveau. But other devices, such as letters of the alphabet formed from the shape of human bodies and deliberate calculation of line and form to evoke mood, lean away from "art for art's sake" to a search for novelty on the one hand and conscious perceptual control on the other. Two thousand copies were printed; it must have been disappointing that it didn't sell well.[35]

In spite of their shared interests, Kulbin and some of the other modernists did not always get along well. Much later Matiushin accused Kulbin of being "eclectic" and "decadent,"[36] but probably at the time Matiushin merely resented his developing position as painter, patron and publisher. Whatever the reason, at the beginning of the 1909-10 season in Petersburg, Matiushin, Guro, and several other painters (including Shkolnik and Spandikov, who appear now to leave Kulbin's group) began to organize a rival association of artists. A studio was rented, and plans were laid for an exhibition. The organization was formally registered as the "Union of Youth" in February 1910.[37] But as works began to be accumulated for the exhibition, Matiushin began to have second thoughts about their quality, and finally he and Guro formally withdrew from the group. Plans for the exhibition continued, now with financial backing from the well-to-do painter L. Zheverzheev, who was also president of the organization. The first exhibition of the "Union of Youth" opened in St. Petersburg on the first of March 1910.[38] Kulbin, of course did not participate; he was preparing his own show; neither did Matiushin or Guro. But David and Vladimir Burliuk did, as well as their friends from Moscow, Mikhail Larionov and Natalia Goncharova. Matiushin's fellow student from Tsionglinskii's studio,[39] Vladimir Markov (Waldemars Matvejs) was represented, as were the other original organizers of the "Union," L. Zheverzheev, Shkolnik, Schleifer, Spandikov and Alexandra Exter. All told, the "Union" showed 222 paintings. As usual, *The Golden Fleece* was not impressed; they pointed out that Larionov and Goncharova sent work which for the most part had already been seen at their recent exhibit, and dismissed the remainder of the show as "hopeless dilettantism" and "forced contrivances."[40]

Less than three weeks later Kulbin's new exhibit, "The Triangle," opened in St. Petersburg. Like Kulbin's first exhibit, "Modern Trends," this was a joint exhibition with Burliuk's "Wreath" group, of which Matiushin now seemed to be a member since he showed two "studies" in the "Wreath's" section of the show.[41] The founders of the "Union of Youth," Shkolnik, Schleifer and Spandikov, who had been in Kulbin's "The Impressionists" the previous year, were all conspicuously absent from "The Triangle." Many of the "Impressionist" exhibitors, however, remained with Kulbin and appeared again in the "Triangle," most notably with the well-known painter August I. Baller, and the other contributors to *The Impressionists Studio,* who showed much of the original work for that publication. Kulbin himself exhibited his work for Evreinov's "A Portrayal of Love": *Stylization of Banality, Night of Love,* and *Despair.* A few of the exhibitors, D. Burliuk, Kulbin, and K.V. Dydyshko, appeared in both the "Triangle" and "Wreath" section of the exhibition; the *Studio* group appeared entirely under the aegis of "Triangle"; and the "Wreath" included V. Burliuk, Exter, Kamensky, and Guro. Breshko-Breshkovsky noted quite correctly that "Wreath" was more "left," i.e. more radical, in its artistic style than "Triangle."[42] The exhibition also displayed regional folk sculpture drawn from private collections, and modern furniture. Most controversial of all was a section composed of drawings and autographs of Russian writers.[43]

"The Triangle" opened just at the time of a general uproar among the artistic groups of the two capitals. Alexander Benois, in a series of "Art Letters" published in the Moscow newspaper *Talk (Rech),* indulged in some rather coarse and heavy handed criticism of the "Seventh Exhibition of the Union of Russian Artists" which had moved in February to St. Petersburg from Moscow.[44] With the change of city, the St. Petersburg members of the "Union of Russian Artists," including Benois, were entitled to invite additional exhibitors of their choice, and so works by more than twenty artists were added to the show. Benois' "Letter" of 26 February then began an open attack on many of the Moscow members of the "Union" whom he named and called "rear-guard," "ballast," "tasteless" and "dead." He decried the ugliness of Kuznetsov and the descent into "chaos" of Larionov and Yakulov. When some of those publicly attacked protested with a hand-delivered letter to Benois, he attempted to have them expelled from the organization. The wrangle dragged on all spring and resulted—in the fall—in the withdrawal of the St. Petersburg group into a newly resurrected "World of Art."[45]

David Burliuk, although he was not in the "Union" exhibition and only mentioned indirectly by Benois in some patronizing and ironic remarks about "Triangle" and "Wreath," flew to the defense of Benois' victims, especially Larionov, Yakulov, and Kuznetsov, and repudiated Benois' compromisingly faint praise. Burliuk sent a personal letter to Benois on 3 March;[46] on 4 April, the night before the closing of "The Triangle" and after the publication of all the letters, he distributed to visitors to the exhibition an open but anonymous answer to Benois. This document was distributed without Kulbin's knowledge and printed by Larionov in the final issue of *The Golden Fleece* at the end of April, but without Burliuk's name; it was instead ascribed to S. Gorodetsky, a prominent participant in "The Triangle."[47]

Meanwhile Kamensky had brought his friend Khlebnikov to meet Matiushin and Guro.[48] The cast was thus assembled for the first literary venture of the new group: a small book with the ambiguous name (invented by Khlebnikov), *Sadok Sudei.* Gathered in Kamensky's and Khlebnikov's apartment, Matiushin, Guro and her sister Ekaterina Nizen, the three Burliuks, Alexander Gorodetsky[49] and Matiushin's mathematician friend S. Masoedov[50] set out to produce a literary almanac so scandalous as to be a "bomb"[51] amongst the more reactionary intelligentsia and establishment literary circles. There was a sense of mission: "One thing was clear to us: the new ideas in art and their formulation were in our hands," Matiushin reports;[52] and Kamensky says, "We understood very well that with this book we were laying a granite cornerstone as the basis of a 'new epoch of literature'."[53]

But the proceedings did not have the tone appropriate to such a solemn occasion. The group began by slyly resolving to avoid trouble with the censor, which the newspapers would surely try to incite, by printing only "lyrical" material. They then gleefully contemplated the surprise and confusion of the critics and journalists who were used to slick literary publications when they were presented with such strange poetry and stories printed on cheap wallpaper. Witticisms at the expense of the establishment grew cleverer and more biting. As the evening wore on glee turned to hilarity and hilarity to uproar as their imaginations soared to encompass the heights of their imminent success. Khlebnikov demanded that they next construct a canal between the Caspian and the Black Seas, Kamensky shouted something about airplanes and x-rays, and they all excitedly made plans to direct the course of civilization from a supremely isolated island.[54]

But, alas, there were soon down-to-earth problems to deal with. No printer would accept such an assignment. Eventually arrangements were made with the printing press of the German newspaper *Petersburger Zeitung*,[55] and a few hundred copies were finally published at the end of April. But the "bomb" fizzled; hardly anyone at all took the publication seriously enough even to be scandalized. Our "bomb," Matiushin remembers sadly, was taken for "a common children's firecracker."[56] Even David Burliuk at first was disappointed with the booklet. At the beginning of May when he received his copies, he wrote to Matiushin, "My first impression was not favorable—but now I am beginning to like them. . ."[57] Obviously, it was an effort. Perhaps the most recognition, albeit of a rather perverse kind, was accorded to the "wallpaper poets" by the reputable *Apollo* when, in November, it reprinted a few excerpts from the book. They appeared in a section of the journal entitled "Bees and Wasps," which consisted mainly of funny selections from the literary lunatic fringe, quoted without comment.[58]

One may wonder whether the formation of the "Union of Youth" and the publication of *Sadok Sudei* had been inspired by news of the Italian Futurists, but there is no evidence to support this idea. Speaking about this time in his memoirs, Matiushin says,

> Did we know at that time about Italian Futurism? We knew, although very little. News about the new art had reached us from France.
> We heard something about Van Gogh and Cezanne in the years 1904-1906, and after two years about French Cubism, and after that also about Italian Futurism.

In the winter of 1910 I was at Shchukin's in Moscow and he showed me Picasso's work, which hung above the pictures of another Spaniard, Zuloaga. . . .[59]

Matiushin probably remembers correctly, for while there had been descriptions of the Italian movement in the Russian press, up until then they had not been very thorough, and, of course, no works were reproduced for there was little yet available. Marinetti's first manifesto had appeared almost immediately in a St. Petersburg newspaper, and this was followed slightly later by an article about "the new literary school." The February 1910 issue of *Apollo* carried a short article by Paolo Buzzi about the arts in Italy, which mentions Futurism and its creator, "G.T. Marinett." In the July-August issue, however, Buzzi, who was Marinetti's friend and collaborator, reproduced, almost in its entirety, the "Technical Manifesto of Painting." Buzzi omits the introductory paragraphs, the names of the signatories, and resorts to paraphrases in several places; but the document is essentially complete. In the same article Buzzi reviews the poetry of Cavacchioli, Lucini, and Palazzeschi and the dramatic work of Maschino, Moselli and Benelli. Buzzi's article is followed by another, describing recent performances in Florence of "La Cena delle Beffe" and "Amore dei tre Re," and including descriptions of the stage sets. A third article, "The Futurists" by Mikhail Kuzmin, mentions *Poesia* and its contributors, and comments dryly and condescendingly on such aspects of the Futurist program as its rejection of the nude and its nationalism.[60]

Thus by late in the summer of 1910 the two most noted Futurist manifestos were available in Russian, and the Russian art world had some knowledge of the movement from the press, although probably a great deal more from personal reports from Western Europe. But this information was still only a very minor current in the news from the West. It had to be assimilated simultaneously with reports from France and Germany (at this time Kandinsky was writing *Apollo's* "Letter from Munich") and all incorporated into the very healthy and lively native interest in modernism.

Perhaps one of the reasons that Matiushin had so readily withdrawn from the "Union of Youth" show was that he knew he would be represented in a much larger and more prestigious show soon to appear in St. Petersburg. Four of his landscapes[61] were being exhibited with the international "Salon" organized by the sculptor Vladimir Izdebsky. This was an enormous exhibition for Russia— almost 800 paintings—which opened in Odessa at the beginning of December 1909, and from there went to Kiev, St. Petersburg, and Riga.[62] Izdebsky, who knew Kandinsky well and had been present at the founding of the "New Artists Federation" in Munich the previous year, wanted to display all of the "new tendencies" in European art on a broad and international scale. For the first time the Russian public would see a large collection of the most recent trends. The weight of the exhibition was given to the French: there were a great many

Expressionists, including Georges Braque, Marie Laurencin, Maurice de Vlaminck, Henri-Charles Manguin, Van Dongen, Albert Marquet, Othon Friesz and Matisse;[63] the Parisian progressive symbolists, associated at the time with the journal *The Golden Veil*—Albert Gleizes, Jean Metzinger, and Le Fauconnier;[64] Paul Signac, the Scientific Impressionist, and his follower and signer of the Futurist manifesto, Giacomo Balla;[65] and other representatives of international modernism. The Munich group included Vasilii Kandinsky, Alexei Javlensky, Gabriele Munter, Marianna Verevkina, and Vladimir Bekhteev.[66]

One wonders how the selections were made amongst the Russian artists. Alexandra Exter had traveled extensively in the West and knew many people, including Izdebsky; perhaps it was she who recommended her friend Matiushin. At the Odessa showing Larionov was represented, but not Goncharova—Lentulov, but not the Burliuks.[67] Kulbin was present only as the subject of a painting—a portrait by Lentulov. Nikolai Tarkhov, the most European of the Russian painters, showed seven pictures; a few works by Bakst and Bilibin represented the new St. Petersburg establishment.

Vladimir and David Burliuk saw the exhibition while it was still in Odessa. "The exhibition is very interesting," David wrote to Kulbin, "there are so many nice French—fine Van Dongen, Braque, Rousseau, Vlaminck, Mangen and many others . . . We came out to the country to work a little before January—I want to terribly (after the French) . . . From Jan. 2-6 we will be in Petersburg and we hope to arrange, under your guidance, the "Impressionists" . . . (the Wreath and △ groups)."[68]

By the time the exhibition arrived in St. Petersburg—at the end of a beautiful warm Russian April and at the height of a new craze for airplanes—Goncharova and the Burliuks had been added to the exhibit and work recently shown in Petersburg had been removed.[69] The "Salon" was not a financial success (in Petersburg the public was too busy with the flying exhibitions to look at paintings), and *The Golden Fleece* jealously called it "an ignorant (illiterate) and disorderly bazaar"[70]; yet such an extensive review of recent continental work could not have been other than a legitimization of Russian modernism in general,[71] and an inspiration to further stylistic explorations. The modernist poet Benedikt Livshits recalls this exhibition as a crucial experience:

> Izdebsky's exhibition played a decisive role in changing my artistic taste and outlook. It not only taught me to *see* a painting—all paintings, even a classical one, which before that I, like the overwhelming majority, used to perceive superficially, like a Cook's tour, but it also brought me to painting, so to speak, from "inside," from the point of view of the problems before the contemporary artist.
>
> It was not only a new vision of the world in all its sensual splendor and startling diversity, past which even yesterday I had gone indifferently, simply without noticing it, it was in addition a new philosophy of art, a heroic esthetics, subverting all the established canons and revealing distances which took my breath away . . .

How to transfer this new experience, these as yet unestablished methods of work, into the sphere of Russian verse, I, of course, did not know and could not know, but I firmly believed that the light came only from there, from the shores of the Seine, from the happy land of liberated painting.[72]

Further exposure of Western painting and some of the more sophisticated Russian work came also from a large and cosmopolitan exhibition organized in Moscow. Aristarkh Lentulov's move to Moscow in connection with his marriage to a well-to-do Moscow woman provided favorable circumstances for mounting the "Jack of Diamonds" exhibition.[73] Like Izdebsky's "Salon," its stylistic center of gravity derived from new movements in the West. Although the initial and monetary impetus came from Lentulov, Larionov became its primary organizer.[74] The name for the exhibition—a more literal translation of the Russian would be "Fool's Knave"—was chosen by Larionov and Lentulov for its ridiculous sound and in opposition to the 'pretty' names—"Blue Rose," "World of Art"—of other associations. "The worse the better, and what can be more preposterous than 'Fool's Knave'," Lentulov wrote.[75] "Jack of Diamonds," which opened in December of 1910, displayed the work of the Munich Russian colony, Kandinsky, Bekhteev, Javlensky, Verevkina and Munter; the French Symbolists and Expressionists, Gleizes, Moreau, Le Fauconnier; and among the Russian adherents of the new movements, Lentulov, Exter, Falk, Konchalovsky, Mashkov, the Burliuks, Larionov and Goncharova. It is notable that most of the Russian exhibitors had studied—or at least visited for some time—in Paris.[76]

One prominent exception to this general circumstance was an exhibitor who sent three works to the "Jack of Diamonds," Kazimir Severinovich Malevich. A provincial painter of Polish parentage from the Southern Ukraine, Malevich had never been outside of Russia,[77] and had been in Moscow since 1902. He had attended the Moscow School of Painting, Sculpture and Architecture and the Stroganov School; from 1907 he contributed regularly to the Moscow Artists Society exhibitions.[78] His fellow exhibitors in these large and variegated displays included Larionov, the Burliuks, Aleksei Morgunov and Vasilii Kandinsky. The "Jack of Diamonds" exhibit was his first move away from relative anonymity into the ranks of the avant-garde. The three works which he sent to "Jack of Diamonds" —*Bather, Fruit, Maid with Fruit*[79]—are not available in the West, but judging from previous and subsequent work it seems probable that they were in the simplified, color-saturated vigorous style derived from the French Expressionists.

Malevich's participation in the "Jack of Diamonds" was most likely at the invitation of Larionov, but probably he had known many of the artistic "youth" for several years by that time. His "Fauvist" works of 1910 and 1911 bear marked resemblance to the French-inspired work of Larionov,[80] although they are distinguished by a more pronounced interest in rhythm and spatial structure. The sources of Malevich's knowledge of contemporary French work must have been relatively few: the private collections in Russia, especially Shchukin's Matisses, the works shown in Izdebsky's "Salon," reproductions and salons of *The Golden Fleece* and second-hand information from his fellow painters. Nevertheless, the evidence of Malevich's painting of this period (for example, *Greenhouses* or *Chiropodist*) shows the assimilation of French Expressionism into Russia to be relatively complete.

Symptomatic of this stage of the new Russian art is the demise in 1910 of *The Golden Fleece*,[81] and the absence of French works from Izdebsky's second exhibition, "Salon 2." Dedicated to the young Russian art which "has found full-bloodedness and strength and has become the only vital and promising art," "Salon 2" opened in Odessa in December of 1910 almost simultaneously with "Jack of Diamonds" in Moscow. Virtually the entire Russian section of the "Jack of Diamonds" (with the exception of Malevich and Morgunov) was represented in Izdebsky's exhibit.[82] In addition it showed work by Kulbin, Dydyshko, Matvejs (Markov), Tatlin, and, of course, the Munich Russians.[83]

The elaborate exhibition catalogue contained essays, poetry and newspaper reviews of the previous "Salon." A bombastic "Introduction" denounced Impressionism and Neo-Impressionism and declared that the "art of yesterday, the art of the weak-willed slaves to nature, has fallen beneath the impassive and inexorable broom of death." Izdebsky defined the task of the new art as "the synthesis of line and form"; in an essay heavily indebted to Nietzsche, "The City of the Future," he maintained that painting is just as musical as tragedy, and that all art and even life itself is in the process of being reborn in the epic and heroic rhythms of a newly harmonious city.

> The soul of the future art and the soul of the future man are born out of the soothing rhythm of the city, and this unique rhythm will sound harmoniously both in souls and in beauty. Man will stop being urban; in the very depths of the city he will be madly close to the earth, to nature, to the sun. Through the city he will sense his lost connection with the life of the world, and religiosity and mysticism will again return to his world view.[84]

Kandinsky attributes similar spiritual significance to the new art in an essay "Content and Form" and in his commentary on his translation of Arnold Schönberg's "Parallels in Octaves and Fifths."[85] Without doubt, readers of the catalogue for "Salon 2" received quite a complete presentation of the Russian version of Western European Expressionism in music, art, poetry and philosophy. From this time forward the Munich group became substantially influential for the new Russian art.

Although news about Italian Futurism must have continued to filter into Russia, there is little evidence that it had any major impact during 1910 and most of 1911. Some assessment of the current avant-garde artistic interests at this time can be made by considering the papers and discussions which took place at the "All Russian Congress of Artists" held in December 1911.[86] Kulbin's major paper, "Harmony, Dissonance and Close Combinations in Art and Life," was illustrated with paintings and musical works and amounted to an up-to-date exposition of his theory of free art. He repeats his belief that everything partakes of potential life and a universal psyche, and that life becomes actual as its structure becomes complicated and disharmonious. If art is to affect man directly, he says, it must be made dissonant to match the complexity and dissonance of the soul or psyche. Its aim is effective transmission of subliminal sensation. It is obvious from this latest version of his theory that Kulbin is familiar with the theoretical formulations of Neo-Impressionism and Symbolism, and that he has adopted the belief that the new art attempts "to penetrate into essence." The concept of physical and psychological equivalents, probably from Helmholtz and Denis, appears quite clearly:

> In art great simplification is necessary together with attention to valuable, characteristic details.... the artist depicts not only color and forms, but also all those important signs of an object which are necessary for the transmission of a poetic experience.[87]

Another source of material for Kulbin is apparently *Matter and Memory* by Bergson, whose fundamental premise of a psychological durée now becomes part of the new "Impressionism."

> All life, in so far as it is accessible to us, is presented as a chain of memories.
>   The present moment, as it is created, no longer exists, but is past. Those links of memories which are called "the past" precede it.
>   There is nothing which remains. And if we look at some picture, we cannot say that it exists as something fixed. Our impressions exist. The picture is a series of memories. You begin to look at it from some point, going along the lines and colors. You receive a series of impressions which move according to the rhythm which is contained in the drawing and the colors.[89]

The apparent "dissonant" remembered impressions—in music, in painting—are thought by Kulbin to harmonize with the innate psychology of the perceiver.

Thus in many respects the ideas of Kulbin are similar to those of Carra, Russolo and Boccioni of about the same time, yet we have no reason to suppose that the Italians rather than Bergson himself are Kulbin's source. Boccioni, in his introduction to the Bernheim-Jeune Exhibition, "The Exhibitors to the Public," simply says that "the picture must synthesize what one remembers and what one sees"; but even this was not published until several weeks after the Congress. The psychological effect of the movement of the eyes had long been a topic of discussion in German and Russian physiology, an area of knowledge in which Kulbin, a physician, may be assumed to have been at home.

Sergei Bobrov, the representative of "Jack of Diamonds," lectured on "Principles of the New Russian Art." Bobrov considers Cezanne, Gauguin, and Matisse "Purists" since they have shown the way to "pure painting" freed of all "secondary concerns." Purism transmits the "vital individuality, the pictorial idea, and gives the metaphysical pictorial essence of things." Bobrov thus approximates the "Impressionism" of the Petersburg painters. Art, he says, must be an intuitive understanding, and if we consider former painting illusionism, then Purism may be called "visionism." Purism is interested in simplification of form, and in this connection he mentions Cezanne and Picasso; he seems to consider the Cubists a subset of the more general term Purism. At the present time, he notes, the Russian Purists have finished learning from France and are looking to native sources.[89]

The interests of the *Blue Rider*, recently separated from the "New Artists Federation," were represented by Kandinsky's paper "Concerning the Spiritual in Art." Since Kandinsky was busy with the *Blue Rider Almanac* and was unable to be present, Kulbin read the paper in two sessions. It is now impossible to ascertain whether the entire tract was read, which does not seem likely, because it was resolved at the Congress to reprint the entire publication in the *Proceedings,* and this was done. At any rate, Kandinsky's esthetic formulations here are an important part of Russian artistic theory.[90] None of the papers, nor any of the discussions which followed and which are published as part of the *Proceedings,* mention Italian Futurism or any of the Futurists.

The two philosophical interests which dominated the new Russian art at the beginning of 1912 were the search for essence and the effective use in art of the human psyche. The reality so often spoken of was sometimes, though not always, metaphysical. The intangible essence for some was associated with a dynamic or vitalist concept of the cosmos, and these artists were not philosophical idealists, but sought to depict on the canvas the concrete energies, forces, potentials and rhythms which they believed to stand behind the visible world. The interest in the artist's individuality and personality was related to the quest for essential reality, for if the artist were to apprehend the vital forces of either object or cosmos, and to transmit this to the viewer through his work, the process could only be personal and subliminal; the senses gave back only the superficial world of appearances which was similar for everyone. Differences sprang from the "subconscious," "inner necessity," "intuition." Among some Russian artists, especially those connected with the "Union of Youth," art and psyche were so closely associated that the new styles in art seemed indicative of a qualitative change in the human consciousness, an event which had been popularly predicted in Russia since the 1880's.

Such concepts differed in an important way from the old Symbolism, since the artist now looked within, rather than above, for clues to reality, and he dealt with notions which were the basis of the relatively new sciences of psychology and physiology. Most artists spurned the "azure mists of Symbolism" and were annoyed when critics failed to make the distinction. During 1912 and 1913 the outer-inner duality would be resolved by many, including Kandinsky, Malevich and Boccioni.

One element which stands out in the general Russian approach to the problems of the new art is an interest in the irrational and the absurd. By 1912 Mikhail Larionov, and others, had introduced a deliberate "coarseness" to their pictures; *Sadok Sudei* had been printed on cheap wallpaper, and Kulbin was emphasizing "irregularities" in the soul. In the search for essence, the initial interest in the naive and the anti-esthetic now turned to cultivation of the absurd. In the April and June (1912) issues of the *Union of Youth* journal, Vladimir Markov (Waldemars Matvejs) distinguishes between two basic approaches in art: a rational "constructiveness" derived from Greece, and an imaginary and illogical "non-constructiveness" derived from the East and based on "feeling." Basic to "non-constructive" art is the "principle of chance" which, when used at all in European art, is only a point of departure for logical development, but in the "non-constructive" approach is the basic method of procedure. Chance beauty may be produced by play, by letting loose that which is wild, primitive and unconscious in the soul so that the individual instinct and psychology may be expressed unrestrainedly. Art which seems absurd, coarse or feeble may have value by virtue of its relationship to some inner essence. Although the forms of art may not be a direct manifestation of the "I," they are sometimes a synthesis of complex analyses and sensations—the echo of the "creator's inner psychology." Since intuition contains some aspect of fundamental truth, modern artists give expression to their unconscious, wild instincts.[91] Markov's article is clear and prophetic. During the next year such notions will give rise to a uniquely Russian contribution to modernism: *zaum*, the "beyond the mind" or "transrational" principle in poetry and painting.

By late in 1912, probably as a result of the Futurist Exhibition which had opened in Paris early in the year and then made an extensive tour of Europe, Italian Futurism was beginning to have an impact in Russia. Although Cubism still remained a favorite topic for public lectures, Futurism began to be mentioned as the latest metamorphosis of modern styles; articles about Futurism, especially the literary side of the movement, now can be found in the popular press.

For painters, the publication in the April 1912 issue of *Union of Youth* of the introduction to the Paris exhibition catalogue, "Exhibitors to the Public," was probably of particular interest since it contained much that would speak to topics already under discussion in Russia. The emphasis now found in Boccioni's esthetic formulation on the individual intuition and emotion, on the blending of "the painted canvas and the soul of the spectator," on the use of "spots, zones of color which do not correspond to any reality" in order to appeal to the psychological processes of the viewer, must only have confirmed the Russian interest in the psychological mechanisms of artist and viewer. The avant-garde would also have responded affirmatively to the familiar notions of depicting the invisible, the artists' new sensitivity, harmonies composed of dissonances, and the many references to Bergsonian concepts.

David Burliuk went to Western Europe—Germany, France, Switzerland and Italy—between April and June of 1912.[92] Undoubtedly he saw the Futurist Exhibition in Germany, where it was that spring. His interest in Futurism is first mentioned just after his return to Russia, in a letter between two officers of the "Union of Youth": it is reported that Burliuk is proposing a talk in Petersburg, "about the Futurists, the French, the Russians—old and new." Burliuk, the letter continues, has "40-50 lantern slides ready to illustrate his paper."[93] His "A Slap in the Face of Public Taste," a purely (literary) Futurist manifesto, was written in December.[94] Italian Futurism had definitely arrived in Russia.

Malevich, Larionov and Kruchenykh: 1912-1913

The popular success of the first "Jack of Diamonds" exhibition was assured when the most illustrious figure of establishment art, Ilya Efimovich Repin, spat in disgust when he saw the paintings. But after it was over Larionov and David Burliuk had a personal falling out. The bone of contention seems to have been the leadership and organization of the Russian "youth." Larionov's personality, widely acknowledged to be "difficult," probably aggravated the matter; he may simply have resented the Burliuks' prior friendship and growing closeness with the Munich Russians. In any event, early in 1911 Larionov had effectively withdrawn from the Jack of Diamonds, and Burliuk had stepped into his place as organizer. When the group was formally incorporated during the year,[1] it was Burliuk's father who paid for the notary public and treated the signatories—Konchalovsky, Kuprin, Mashkov, Lentulov, and the Burliuks—to a celebration dinner.[2] Konchalovsky became president of the society, Lentulov, secretary.[3] The names of Larionov and Goncharova in this venture are emphatically absent.

Quite early, apparently, Larionov had made some attempt to associate himself with Kandinsky, for there is extant a letter from Kandinsky to Goncharova, dated 1 March 1911, wherein Kandinsky mentions that Larionov has written him about some "publications" and inquires about his "Ass's Tail" society.[4] Furthermore, although it was the Burliuks who exhibited at the first "Blue Rider" exhibition, Kandinsky invited Larionov, Goncharova and Malevich to contribute to the second one of February or March 1912, and they did.[5]

Various alterations of alliances are quite clearly reflected in the make-up of the second "Jack of Diamonds" which opened—after a three week delay due to a shortage of exhibition space in Moscow—at the end of January, 1912.[6] Larionov, Goncharova and their friends, including Malevich and Morgunov, were nowhere to be seen. There are several new representatives from France: Picasso, Matisse (who each sent three items), and Leger (who contributed five). The composition of the Munich group reflects the recent break with Munich New Artists' Federation.[7] Although Javlensky and Verevkina were invited to participate,[8] they did not, nor did Kanoldt and Erbsloh who, although they had appeared in the first "Jack of Diamonds" exhibit, now found themselves in opposition to Kandinsky in Munich. The contributors to the new "Blue Rider" exhibition, however, were admirably represented; in addition to former partic-

ipants in the Jack of Diamonds—Kandinsky, Munter and Le Fauconnier—
Kandinsky's allies Marc, Macke and Kirchner now sent works to Moscow.
A notable addition to the Moscow contingent is Kulbin, Burliuk's old friend
who was growing increasingly close to Kandinsky. This is Kulbin's first pene-
tration into a Moscow exhibition; his listing in the catalogue bears the notation
"St. Petersburg."

In connection with the exhibition, Burliuk arranged evenings of lectures
and debates. For the first, in addition to talks by himself ("On Cubism and
Other New Directions in Painting") and Kulbin ("Free Art as the Basis of Life")
Burliuk planned to present a paper by Kandinsky (probably the one read a
month previously by Kulbin at the Congress), but this apparently did not occur.
(When he visited Munich two months hence, however, Burliuk would invite
Kandinsky himself to speak in Moscow the following season, and Kandinsky,
it seems, agreed.)[9] But Kulbin, Burliuk, and the auspices of the notorious
Jack of Diamonds proved quite enough to pack the large auditorium of the
Polytechnical Museum. Rumors about an explosive clash with Larionov
promised added amusement, and the public response was so enthusiastic that
extra police had to be summoned to turn away disgruntled crowds who could
not fit into the hall.

Burliuk's and Kulbin's presentations went relatively peacefully, the
audience responding only intermittently with the shouts, laughter and catcalls
which had become *de rigueur* at the public appearances of the Russian "youth."
Burliuk's statement that the works of Velasquez and Raphael were nothing
more than "photographs," and the slides shown of "leftist" works, were rather
minor scandals.[10] But the anticipated clash between Larionov's group and the
Jack of Diamonds did materialize and, as expected, created a scandal of larger
proportions. Toward the end of the evening, during a reasonably controlled
discussion by spokesmen from the audience, Goncharova appeared suddenly.
The audience grew silent and alert as she ringingly objected to Kulbin's showing
slides of two of her paintings as examples of the work of Jack of Diamonds. She,
she declared, in fact belonged to "The Ass's Tail!" The house screamed with
laughter.

"There is no reason to laugh at the name."

Goncharova's assertion was so undeniably authoritative that the audience fell
silent again.

"First see the exhibition when it opens—then laugh. To laugh now is ignorant."

Goncharova had so effectively chastized her audience that they listened
without protest to a long *ex-cathedra* speech on the origins of Cubism, its relation to Primitivism and her claim that she had been the first Russian Cubist.

She criticized the Jack of Diamonds for conservatism, excessive theorizing and a lack of emphasis on subject matter.[11] A few days later she repeated her accusations in long letters to several newspapers.[12]

It was a magnificent publicity stunt. When "The Ass's Tail" opened a month later in the exhibition hall of the Moscow School of Painting, Sculpture and Architecture with work by Malevich, Morgunov, Tatlin, Chagall, Matvejs, and Shevchenko,[13] as well as a hundred and ninety seven pieces by Larionov and Goncharova, there was no lack of an audience. Nor was scandal lacking: the administration of the Moscow School, (perhaps still sensitive to the trouble Larionov had caused two years earlier) refused to allow a sign with the inscription "The Ass's Tail" above their entrance; and the censor confiscated Goncharova's paintings of ecclesiastical themes because he suspected it might be sacrilegious to display them at an exhibition with such a name.[14]

But Goncharova had been right. In spite of the exhibition's insolent name, there was no reason to laugh. "The Ass's Tail" must be considered the most serious and substantial exposition of the new Russian art yet assembled. Malevich showed twenty-four works including many 'Fauvist' pieces, some of which— *Argentine Polka, On the Boulevard*—had been shown in Petersburg slightly earlier. Also in this exhibition—obviously recently completed—were studies of peasant groups and individual peasant heads. (It was one such head which Malevich had sent to Kandinsky for the second Blue Rider exhibition going on at the same time in Munich.)[15] The most striking aspect of these peasant works is Malevich's newly subdued pallette; in place of the dominant clear blues, yellows, and reds of his 'Fauvist' works, Malevich had switched to cool greens, and neutral ochres, browns and greys. But the bright expressionist colors were not entirely abandoned, they were retained for emphasis, balance, or to structure facial features. In several cases, faces embedded in a dark group are almost entirely clear yellow or orange.

In retrospect Malevich emphasized that the peasant subject matter, "our people," was the feature which most distinguished himself and Goncharova from the Jack of Diamonds,[16] but at the time, many critics failed to notice any differences at all between the two groups, so varied were the subjects and approaches. Indeed many must have felt as Tugendkhold did when he lumped all the Moscow youth together in one composite group: "Fool's Knaves and Tails."[17]

The development of Larionov's new Rayist style of painting occurred during 1912. At "The Ass's Tail" he showed several "photographic studies"[18] and it is likely that these, probably Futurist in style, engendered the beginnings of Rayist theory. There is no doubt that Larionov was at the time fully aware of Italian Futurism. Goncharova, in one of her letters to the press after the break with Jack of Diamonds, describes Futurism as "emotional Impressionism," and in "The Ass's Tail" she shows works done in the "Futurist style" along with others in "Cubist style," "Chinese style" and so forth. The objections both artists had made about Jack of Diamond's theorizing and lack of emphasis on subject matter were objections an early Futurist might have made to the Cubists. Rayism is a latter day Neo-Impressionism which prescribes the depiction of the interaction of light rays reflected from objects and their environment.[19] Its acknowledged debt to Futurism was the adoption of the ideas of painting what one knows, rather than what one sees, and the rendering of a synthetic sum total of impressions. Yet Larionov shares none of the conceptual conceits of Futurism. Rayism is a physical theory. He means to paint only what *he knows he sees.* Larionov conceived of this process almost as putting the canvas into the air to skim off the light image as it trembled in space like a mirage. The painting is bound only by truly painterly elements, which Larionov reduced to three: color (form and line are left implicit in the color phenomena), texture, and the sensation which arises from their combination. The extremity of these two propositions—the absolute physicality of the phenomena and the reductivist pictorial principles—allows Larionov to maintain a philosophical absolutism whereby objects attain their "most complete reality" only on the canvas. Thus Rayism becomes something more than an artistic style; Larionov dismissed style as "mere fashion." Nor was Rayism limited to measurable radiation; even that given off by thought or by strong emotion might be captured on the canvas. "There are reasons to suppose," Larionov wrote, "that the whole world in its concrete and spiritual totality can be recreated in pictorial form." For more than a year Larionov did not hesitate to specify the subjects of his apparently objectless paintings because he considered them literal renderings of physical and philosophical fact.

As in Neo-Impressionism and early Futurism, the individuality of the artist was to play a minimal role in Rayism. Larionov repeatedly emphasized this point, and often criticised his fellow Russians for their preoccupation with personality. The principal Russian exponent of Italian Futurism was Ilya Zdanevich, Larionov's good friend and critic.[20] In March of 1913, in connection with Larionov's inauguration of Rayism at his "Target" exhibition, Zdanevich gave a public lecture on "Marinetti's Futurism"; about two weeks later in a lecture about Futurism and Rayism he presented a detailed history of Futurism, read a selection of manifestos, and showed slides of Futurist work.[21] In the second lecture Zdanevich attacked the Russian "Futurists," including Igor Severianin and Velimir Khlebnikov, for their lack of "struggle" and for failing to bring "art into life," a fundamental principle of Futurism. Real Futurism, he said, is not to be found either in the "Jack of Diamonds" or the "Union of Youth"; "only Goncharova and Larionov practise it." But while Zdanevich and Larionov considered Rayism related to Italian Futurism, they also considered it a particularly Russian manifestation of it. Certainly they were not averse to borrowing freely from the Italian polemic and adding a Russian orientation: "We demand patriotism and love of Russia," Zdanevich ended his talk, "but Russia is Asia and we are proud of this. . . . We are the last barbarians of the old world and the first of the new."[22]

Larionov's program to bring "art into life" began in the fall and consisted of leading his disciples in strolls about the streets of Moscow, their faces painted with Rayist designs. The "Manifesto of the Futurists" which he and Zdanevich published at the very end of 1913 is directly in the Italian tradition. It begins with a vision of the "frenzied city" and maintains throughout its four pages a happy forthrightness and vivacity; probably it was written by Zdanevich.

> To the frenzied city of arc lamps, to the body spattered streets squeezing the houses, we brought a painted face: the start is given and the course awaits the runners. . . .
>
> We have linked art with life. After the artists' long seclusion we called life loudly, and life invaded art; it is time for art to invade life. Painting the face is the beginning of the invasion. . . .
>
> We, creators, have nothing to do with the earth, our lines and colors originated with us.
>
> If we were given plumage like a parrot, we would pluck out the feathers for the sake of brushes and pencils. . . .
>
> Mutiny against the earth and the transformation of faces in the projector of experience.
>
> The telescope discerned constellations which had been forgotten in space; our painting recounts forgotten thoughts.
>
> We paint ourselves—because a clean face is repulsive, because we want to herald the mysterious; we are remaking life and we bear to the upper reaches of existence the multiplied soul of man.[23]

A laconic note appended by the editor observes in part: "Futurism migrated to us from the West and, finding prepared ground among the 'radical left' of Russian art, quickly located its leaders and prophets." Beneath their photographs Larionov and Goncharova are each described as "Head of the Futurists."

It is difficult to assess just how much influence Futurist painting may have had on Larionov's Rayism. The most likely date for its development is late 1912, after the Paris Exhibition. Thus he may have seen such works as Boccioni's *The Forces of a Street* or Carra's *The Movement of the Moonlight,* indeed he probably did, if only in Zdanevich's photographic reproductions. But while his interest in Rayism lasted, Larionov's conception of his work and the paintings themselves went quickly to greater extremes than the Futurism of the time, or for that matter than Orphism. It seems most likely that Larionov arrived at Rayism by way of his own Impressionist work and early Futurist theory, and, as befitted his personality, he plunged headlong into its most uncompromising expression. In spite of some of their polemical statements to the contrary, both Larionov and Zdanevich were strongly oriented toward the West. For Larionov especially, acknowledgment by the Western art world was important.

When Futurism became popular in Russia, he simultaneously had to assert the orthodoxy of his Futurism in his rejection of Russian "imitations," and maintain the "Russianness" of his innovation in the eyes of Westerners. Rayism had to be established as the only direct, but thoroughly Russian, descendant of the Italian movement, as well as a radically new absolute art. It was probably this point of view that Larionov wished to propagate in the proposed second *Blue Rider Almanac.*[24]

Malevich continued to be associated with Larionov's group, and consequently was also aware of the progress of Italian Futurism, until the "Target" exhibition in March of 1913. This exhibition, which first set forth the Rayist program, is notable also for its introduction of new work by Malevich apparently related to Western Futurism. *The Knife Grinder* is a highly successful study based on a cubist fragmentation of the motion of grinding wheel and figure; another work, *Dynamic Splitting,* may have been a similar representation of motion. In *Morning in the Village After the Snowfall* figures and landscape are resolved into patterned cubic and triangular shapes. These works seem to have been something of experiments for Malevich, and both are elaborations of his method of rendering figures as simplified volumetric forms, his "New Russian Style" which he had introduced just three months earlier.[25] The subjects for all of these paintings are still scenes from peasant life which he and Goncharova had concerned themselves with for the past year; but now his canvases have become extremely ordered, the space sharply divided into planar distances, the modelling of the figures created by strips of color. Apparently Malevich had developed this style during the second half of 1912, that is, while Larionov was developing Rayism and after the Paris Futurist exhibition.

Immediately before the "Target" exhibition Larionov broke off with his friends at the "Union of Youth." The Union had been prepared to sponsor a public lecture by him at the beginning of March about Rayism, but he withdrew abruptly when Burliuk, Kruchenykh, and the other Cubo-Futurist poets became allied officially with the Unionists. Malevich, however, had also been invited to speak under Union auspices, and he did so, which undoubtedly caused hard feelings with his old friend Larionov. Malevich gave his lecture in Petersburg at the same time that Zdanevich was speaking on "Marinetti's Futurism" in Moscow. Both lectures were given on 23 March 1913, the evening before "Target" opened.[26]

By July, Larionov's feelings were quite apparent. In his book *The Donkey's Tail and Target* he published a review by Varsanofii Parkin which characterized Malevich's 1911 primitivist paintings as

> Large, bright and disorderly watercolors, with a sickly, indifferent expression of the figures and with that nasty Polish style with which the things of Vrubel abound.

About the "Target" pieces he said:

> This year [Malevich] has devoted himself to a shallow cubism mixed with graphic painting of various motifs from agricultural life. The things are dry, but have a certain technical merit.[27]

Malevich's new association with the "Union of Youth" and in particular with Mikhail Matiushin, who had returned to the "Union" only in November of 1912,[28] and with the Cubo-Futurist poet Alexei Kruchenykh, seems to have had several observable effects. While still pursuing his primary philosophical interest in man's position in an infinite universe, he abandoned the peasant subjects which had been used by Larionov and Goncharova and concerned himself with two of the interests of his new associates: Cubism and the conscious manipulation of stylistic elements for psychological effect.

Kruchenykh had settled in Moscow in the winter of 1910-1911, and in the course of the next year and a half met all of Burliuk's friends, including Khlebnikov and Vladimir Mayakovsky, then an art student at the Moscow School;[29] early in 1912 he gave up painting and began to write poetry. At a debate at the closing of the second "Jack of Diamonds" exhibition, he and Mayakovsky acted as "opponents" to Burliuk and Max Voloshin.[30] Kruchenykh also managed to maintain friendly relations with Larionov and Goncharova. His first poetic work, *Game in Hell*, (written in collaboration with Khlebnikov) was published in the summer of 1912 with Goncharova's illustrations. She and Larionov and Tatlin continued to illustrate all of Kruchenykh's works until his alliance with the Union of Youth.[31]

Although the formal alliance of Burliuk's little group of writers (Benedikt Livshits, Khlebnikov, Kruchenykh, Mayakovsky, and, of course, the Burliuks themselves) with the "Union" had made Larionov angry enough to cancel his paper on Rayism in St. Petersburg and to break with Kruchenykh, it also brought about the most creative period and the most fertile associations in the history of the new Russian art. As *The Golden Fleece* had earlier brought Post-Impressionist and progressive Symbolist ideas into Russia, the three issues of the *Union of Youth* journal energetically propagated the more advanced Western schools as well as Eastern art and poetry. Smaller and much less lavish than *The Golden Fleece*, it concerned itself more with philosophical and theoretical problems. In its three issues—published in April and June of 1912 and March 1913 (this last issue with the Cubo-Futurists)—it printed, among many other things, Markov's long and important essay "Principles of the New Art," the Futurist "Technical Manifesto of Painting" and "Exhibitors to the Public" from the Bernheim-Jeune catalogue, Le Fauconnier's statement about his work, Elie Faure's essay on Van Dongen and Van Dongen's letters from the *Catalogue for the "Second Exhibit of the New Artists Federation,"* and Matiushin's excerpted translations from Gleizes and Metzinger's *Du Cubisme*. The propagation of the new art from Europe, coupled with interests which had been developing in Russia since 1908, combined to make a rich intellectual medium for the three men who now found themselves allied for the first time—Matiushin, from the "Union of Youth," Malevich from "The Ass's Tail" and Kruchenykh from the literary "Hylea."[32] From this association, directly or indirectly, came Kruchenykh's theory of the "self-sufficient word" and *zaum*,[33] Matiushin's life-long study of the notions of color and space,[34] and Malevich's Suprematism. In December 1913 they produced Russia's first absurdist spectacle, the opera "Victory Over the Sun."

The single most important aspect of Cubo-Futurist esthetics for modernism was its concern with psychology. Although Kruchenykh condemned symbolist "psychologizing"[35] and declared the word to be "self-sufficient," he never concealed his interest in the psychological basis of his own literary style. He disliked the Symbolist search for correspondence, the desire to manipulate, on any level, the consciousness of the perceiver, and regarded any calculated appeal to the subliminal, even to subconscious associations, as just a further extension of the kind of lock-step logic of rational thought he sought to avoid.[36] To Kruchenykh, the self-sufficiency of the word derived from its independence from logic, from grammar, from the "real" world, and thus it was left free to demonstrate the bare bone of the psyche. Any theory of art, Nikolai Kulbin had said in 1910, must be derived from "nature as reflected in the psyche of the artist."[37] This was the only reality truly (and just barely) accessible to the artist. The Cubo-Futurists' exploration of primitive and child art was motivated by their desire to get at the human brain as a piece of the universe, untouched by learned logic; but in the psyche Kulbin had discerned not "harmony," which he defined as correct relationships, symmetry, sleep, dormancy, but a certain "dissonance," which accompanies any complication of form. Kulbin had suggested that dissonance—in form, in color, in tone—had affective value because, "In man's nature there are irregularities *(nepravil'nosti)* . . . and so complete harmony will not suit him."[38] Three years later, in *The Declaration of the Word as Such,* Kruchenykh repeated Kulbin: "In art there may be unresolved dissonances 'unpleasant to hear' for in our soul there is a dissonance to which they are resolved."[39] This demand that language be the objectification of a psychological realm which is dissonant or irregular or complicated led Kruchenykh inevitably to his "beyond the mind" language, *zaum.*

The desire to encompass a vital, intuitive, but seemingly chaotic relationship with the universe made even chance a positive device in the new art. Far from finding uncertainty a destructive force which undermines the meaning of life, the Cubo-Futurists were charmed by accidental occurrences, by typographical errors for example; they were the occasion for rejoicing, because they made manifest those all-pervasive natural laws which link man with nature. Vladimir Markov in his essay "Principles of the New Art" published in the

Union of Youth journals of 1912 elevated chance to an artistic principle and pointed to Chinese pottery glazes and wind chimes as examples. Markov also mentioned another very important aspect of the new art—its absurd nature: "To be ugly and absurd on the outside does not mean to possess no inner values," he writes, and "often it seems that the absurd forms are not the echo and translation of Nature, but the echo of the creator's inner psychology. " 'They are the swans of other worlds,' as the Chinese sing."[40] The absurdity of Kruchenykh's works was a very specific *zaum* behavior; it was different from the *seemingly* absurd with a hidden message, an apparent lack of sense which disappears when the right key or keys are found, different even from the "surreal" type of subconscious associations. This absurdity was a mindless, irresolvable condition meant only to reveal new and heretofore invisible realms, those "swans of other worlds." The breakdown of causality which will be found in *Victory Over the Sun* is an appeal to a higher cause, one that is implicit only in the form of the work itself. It is in this sense that it may be called "self-sufficient." The spatial-temporal coherence is destroyed for the sake of a simultaneous universe, one that is stable and pervasive.

In a programmatic statement published six months before the performance of *Victory*, Kruchenykh and Malevich were to state their intention to destroy thought which moves according to the laws of logic and causality, and "to transmit a personal creative insight into the genuine world of the new people."[41] This "genuine world of the new people" refers to a concept which had been developing in Russia ever since the late nineteenth century. Since the new psychology had postulated physiologically based sense perceptions, it seemed reasonable to suppose that at some future time human perception of space and time would evolve—presumably to even greater sensitivity and higher levels of consciousness. P.D. Uspensky published two books which had this as their main thesis: *The Fourth Dimension* in 1909 and *Tertium Organum* in 1911.[42] Both books were well known to Malevich and Kruchenykh (and to the Cubo-Futurists in general). Uspensky is responsible for bringing together and popularizing several non-Russian sources of similar ideas. He quotes at length from *Cosmic Consciousness* by R.M. Bucke, a Canadian physician and a friend of Walt Whitman, and from the work of Edward Carpenter, the English socialist-mystic. Uspensky also seems to have been the primary early source in Russia for Charles Hinton's two books, *A New Era in Thought* and *The Fourth Dimension*,[43] which he quoted extensively in both *The Fourth Dimension* and *Tertium Organum*.

The basic proposition of all these works is similar: that man is developing a new level of perception that will enable him to see and understand the world in a suprasensible way. Bucke follows current physiological arguments to trace the development of the conceptual ability from initial raw sensory data, and projects this process into the future when man will proceed to an even greater capacity for abstraction than he now possesses. Carpenter had a similar scheme. All of these writers, including Uspensky himself, agreed that the new people with the new powers were about to, or had already begun to, appear in society. Uspensky differed from his Western counterparts in that, instead of believing that the new developments would be essentially religious or mystical manifestations, as Bucke and Carpenter suggested, he maintained, following the popular and influential philosopher Vladimir Solovev, that the new consciousness would first be noticed in art.

> In art we already have the first experience of the *language of the future.* Art is the avant-garde of psychological evolution.
>
> And not in anything else, at the present stage of our development, do we possess such a strong means for knowledge of the causal world as in art.
> The artist must be clear seeing, he must see that which others do not see. . . .[44]

"We are the new people of the new life!" The Cubo-Futurists lost no time in declaring themselves the new men and their art the "art of the future."[45] By the art of the future they meant two things: that their art was stylistically avant-garde, and that it was also in the psychic avant-garde, that it somehow gave a glimpse, an impression, of future mental capacities. They did not mean this in a mechanistic way (i.e. that this is what things would 'look like') but that the new style had a quality or qualities which produced the "sensation" of future consciousness. It was this nebulous "sensation" which they called the "fourth dimension."

This term was apparently first published in connection with Cubist painting in France by Metzinger in the fall of 1910.[46] But in France even the philosophically inclined Cubists, such as Metzinger, were inclined to apply the ideas of non-Euclidean geometry rather literally to the Cubist understanding of space.[47] As a matter of fact, in order to better understand the new art, some painters did actually attempt a serious study of mathematics. In Russia the idea of a fourth dimension caught and spread because it expressed in one phrase an important element in the milieu from which modernism in art emerged. It was a concept which embodied a happy combination of science and philosophical idealism. It seemed to prove the notion, given common currency by the Symbolists, that what is visible is not necessarily real (the Symbolists often pointed out that matter was really mostly space and energy), and was somehow mystically emblematic of the twentieth century and the scientific age. The idea of a new dimension, understood, however vaguely, as having to do with space and time, made all of Western art instantly passé.

The conservative critic Sergei Makovsky, in a review of the *Union of Youth* journal of March 1913, gave one explanation of the "fourth dimensional" approach to Cubism and Futurism:

There is in every three dimensional object the possibility of numberless positions in space. But to perceive this series of positions ad infinitum the artist can only conform to the various moments of time (for example, going around an object or setting it in motion). Consequently, at a given moment an object is always imagined in some single position, i.e., not moving in time. This proceeds from the fact that the artist himself moves in time, i.e., he is in the fourth dimension. . . . If, mentally, one goes out of time, i.e., becomes as it were above time, becomes unmoving in time, then just the opposite results. There occurs a mental instability of the object itself in time (a numberless series of its positions at one time for the contemplating artist), the object is not in three but four dimensions which may be expressed graphically by putting into one space (in this case the picture plane) that series of positions of the object (even if fragmentary and of course only to a certain approximation) for it is impossible to picture numberlessness. One may clearly imagine an object moving in space, for example, a wheel. What is the movement of a wheel if not a numberless series of positions at various moments in time? You "stop time" and these positions are combined, as it were, come together (because the wheel is one thing) and we no longer get a three dimensional wheel, but a wheel in the "fourth dimension."

Furthermore, to imagine this mathematical form of the wheel visually it remains only for the artist to show in the picture the multiplicity of positions as if he were unwinding a movie film (of course, to the extent that is necessary to stimulate the associative activity of our brain). Many futurist paintings illustrate this example very graphically. Other cases of this "graphic multiplicity" portray the motion not of the object but around the object or inside the object or a combination of these motions. For example, the famous "violin" of Picasso belongs to the last category of "four dimensional portrayal."[48]

Unfortunately this kind of mechanistic explanation for the multiple viewpoints of early Cubism and the Futurists' efforts to depict motion was more acceptable to the public who needed a guide to the seeming irrationality of the canvas than to the artists themselves. Malevich, in one of his first public statements, cautioned against this kind of rigid, rationalist interpretation: "I give warning of a danger. Reason has now imprisoned art in a box of square dimensions. . . ."[49] In the introduction to *The Three (Troe)*, a small collection of poems published in September of 1913,[50] Matiushin equates this type of reasoning with the third dimension, thus implying the qualities of the fourth:

> The days are not far when the conquered phantoms of three-dimensional space, of the illusory drop-shaped time, and of the cowardly causality . . . will reveal before everybody what they really have been all the time—the annoying bars of a cage in which the human spirit is imprisoned.[51]

In fact, it was just the impossibility of conceiving of the fourth dimension, its nebulousness, its susceptibility to various interpretations, that made it an appropriate allegory for the science-induced euphoria of the times. In *The Cubist Painters* Apollinaire had not quite successfully grasped at this feeling:

> Regarded from a plastic point of view, the Fourth Dimension appears to spring
> from the three known dimensions: it represents the immensity of space externalizing
> itself in all directions at any given moment. It is space itself, the dimension of the
> infinite; the Fourth Dimension endows objects with plasticity. It gives the object its
> right proportions on the whole, whereas in Greek art, for instance, a somewhat
> mechanical rhythm constantly destroys the proportions. . . .[52]

Thus the *Union of Youth* journal mentions its "fight against the mechanical
and temporal" and "the broadening of the estimation of what is beautiful
beyond the limits of consciousness (the principle of relativity)"[53] among the
distinguishing characteristics of their new art.

Like the French Cubists, the Russian painters also appreciated the simplicity and the unconscious truths revealed in folk and primitive art; but Russian
modernism proceeded not from the idea that Cubism gave new conventions of
rendering the visible world, but that it was a means of describing that which was
not immediately perceptible. Primitive art seemed a "more perfect" revelation
both of the individual artist, of human nature itself, and even of a "divine"
principle. The artist is a "creator" not a "spy," the Union of Youth artists said
in 1913, and indeed it seems doubtful whether in Russia Cubism was ever felt
to be strongly related to the visible world.[54]

Gleizes and Metzinger had also associated the Cubist style with an indi-
vidualistic psychology:

> There is nothing real outside ourselves; there is nothing real except the coinci-
> dence of a sensation and an individual mental development. We are far from thoughts
> of doubting the existence of things which strike our senses, but strictly speaking,
> we can have certainty only about those images they give birth to in our minds.[55]

These were ideas familiar enough to the Russian avant-garde. The "world of
appearances" had been in disrepute since before the turn of the century, and
idealism and anti-positivism stood behind every phase of their activities. But
now their approach also had a scientific basis in psychology and physiology,
as the artists themselves often pointed out.

The vision of a new and future world was closely associated with Kruchenykh's ideas about language. Bucke and others have suggested very early that
a change in language would be one of the outward manifestations of the new
consciousness. Kulbin had essentially agreed. "For the depiction of the new and
the future *completely new words and a new combination of them* are necessary," Kruchenykh declared in "New Ways of the Word." "A new content is
only revealed when new devices of expression are attained . . . once there is a
new form there is consequently a new content . . . form causes content," and
vice versa. "The psyche gives birth to strange senseless combinations of words
and letters," and these in turn produce "a new perception of the world."[56]
In *Declaration of the Word as Such*, he explained, "By creating new words I

bring in a new content where everything begins to slip (the conventions of time and space, etc., here I agree with Kulbin . . .)."[57] Kruchenykh lists various devices which will generate the slipping in space and change in perception: incorrect sentence structure, grammatical confusions, neologisms, unexpected sound patterns, and also absurd action, strange comparisons and primitive coarseness.

Malevich at this time develops an absurd, alogical style in painting. One of his devices is a variation in the size of objects which does not depend on any systematic perspective. There is also little or no narrative cohesion in a work; unrelated and incongruous images simply turn the mind back on itself until interpretation is abandoned. In *Woman at the Tram Stop* a man, not a woman, appears peering from behind one of the painting's rectangular planes, and a realistically painted bottle and schedule occupy central positions in an otherwise objectless, cubistically constructed work. *The Aviator* shows a huge fish partially covering the body of a one-eyed man, and scattered letters of the word "drugstore" *(apteka)* add to the puzzle. In "New Ways of the Word" Kruchenykh mentioned incorrect perspective as one means of inducing his more transcendent universe,[58] and in *Englishman in Moscow* we find Malevich also experimenting with this idea. In addition to the absurd fish and a red spoon stuck onto the Englishman's hat, a tiny ladder is contrasted with a sword as wide as the painting, and a church, complete with cupolas and crosses, appears in front of, and smaller than, the man's face. The viewer is refused his usual point of view outside of the painting and is forced, like Alice, merely to accept an ambiguous position in a topsy turvy world of objects which do not behave properly. Because they do not obviously relate to one another, except of course as structural parts of the composition, the viewer is compelled to accept each one individually as a "self-sufficient object." There is a curious coincidence of Kruchenykh's terms and Malevich's images here: Kruchenykh wrote, "We think that language should first of all be *language,* and if it reminds one of anything then it should be a saw or the poisoned arrow of a savage." A saw juts out from behind the hat of Malevich's Englishman, and a large red arrow sweeps across his chest.

The sets designed by Malevich for *Victory* work out the analogies drawn by Kruchenykh between the methods of futurist poets and painters. Just as Kruchenykh derived his *zaum* language from the splintering and reordering of words, Malevich here began to slice objects apart. It is important to note that he was not concerned with reducing or simplifying or idealizing the object, but simply with showing partial views, cross sections and distortions of perspective. "We have cut the object!" Kruchenykh cried, "We have begun to see through the world!"[59] The operative process can be seen clearly by comparing two paintings: *The Woodcutter,* and one of the many latter works designated without reference to a subject, *Suprematist Composition* (1917). The logs and figure of the earlier painting appear in the later one as plane sections. The wood-cutter is still bent over his task, a ghostly shadow of his other life. Unlike the Cubists, Malevich never hesitated to abandon all overt references to the objects of the real world, in spite of the fact that his geometrical elements derived directly from them. Nor did he insist on the Cubists' flat spatial perspective; although some works are entirely coincident with the picture plane, many others display traditional perspective, and some have a deep, cosmic sense of space.

Three of Malevich's favorite stylistic devices—partial view, alteration of size, and the substitution of flat planes for rounded surfaces—were developed during this period, but possibly the immediate impetus toward the new style was the experiments with light in the production of *Victory*. It is not *new* objects which should be used in art, Kruchenykh had said, but a new and fantastic light should be thrown upon the old ones.[60] As we shall see, Malevich adopted this statement quite literally in *Victory;* spotlights roamed the stage during the performance, picking out and focusing attention on random pieces of bodies and backdrops. On the backdrops themselves, painted light often seems to come from strange angles, distorting objects beyond recognition and casting long and mysterious shadows. The role of these shadows can be seen clearly in an illustration from *Troe,* the publication in which Kruchenykh's "New Ways of the Word" appeared. Since modeling with light has been abandoned, the planar divisions have become either bright or dark, and the independent "suprem-atist" elements have begun to emerge. This illustration is one of the most striking demonstrations of Malevich's route to the new objectless world.

Victory Over the Sun: December 1913

In July 1913, Malevich spent some time in Uusikirkko, Finland with Kruchenykh and Matiushin, who was recovering from his wife's untimely death two months previously. Khlebnikov, summering in Astrakhan with his parents, had intended to accompany the other three. "I am coming," he wrote to Matiushin. "Wait for me and send me 18-20 roubles, those earthly wings, to fly from Astrakhan to you."[1] But no sooner had he received the money from Matiushin than he dropped it into the water while bathing and lost it. "The purse slipped away as if it were alive. . . . Later I tried to fish for the purse-frog with a hook and line, but nothing came of it," he wrote sorrowfully to Matiushin.[2]

While in Uusikirkko, Kruchenykh worked on the libretto for *Victory Over the Sun.* "I wrote *Victory Over the Sun* imperceptibly," Kruchenykh noted later; "the stimulus of the very unusual voice of Malevich and the gentle singing violin of dear Matiushin helped me to formulate it."[3] On 18 and 19 July, Malevich, Kruchenykh, and Matiushin held a conference which they rather grandly called "The First All-Russian Congress of Poets of the Future (The Poet-futurists)." Their program and stylistic intentions were soon proclaimed in *During the Last 7 Days:*

CHRONICLE
The First All-Russian Congress of Poets of the Future [The Poet-futurists].
A meeting on the 18th and 19th of July, 1913, in Uusikirkko (Finland).

The kind of activities for the coming year are being discussed and planned, activities of the year which is ending are examined, and papers are given; D. Burliuk's, Khlebnikov's "On the New Music," and others.

In general the plans and ideas are expressed in the following precepts:

We intend to arm the world against us!

The time of slaps is passed:

The noise of explosion and the slaughter of scarecrows will rock the coming year of art!

We want our opponents bravely to ban the scattering of their belongings! Let them not wag their tails and not be able to hide themselves behind them. We commanded with a crowd of thousands at meetings and in theaters and from the pages of our clear books, and now we shall announce the rights of singers and artists, lacerating the ears of those vegetating under the stump of cowardice and immobility:

1) To destroy the "clean, clear, honest, resonant Russian language" emasculated and smoothed out by the tongues by the man from "criticism and literature."

It is unworthy of the great "Russian people!"

2) To destroy the antiquated movement of thought according to the law of causality, the toothless, common sense, the "symmetrical logic" wandering about in the blue shadows of Symbolism and to give the personal creative enlightenment of the real world of the new people.

3) To destroy the elegance, frivolousness, and beauty of cheap public artists and writers; constantly issuing newer and newer works in words, in books, on canvas and paper.

4) With this aim, about the first of August of this year new books are taking off: *Three* by Khlebnikov, Kruchenykh and E. Guro, *Illus.* by K. Malevich; *Heavenly Baby Camels* by E. Guro; *Croaked Moon* by the collaborators of "Hylea"—*Print and We* and others.

5) To swoop down on the stronghold of artistic weakness—on the Russian theater and decisively to reform it.

There is no room today! For the Art Theater, the Korshevsky, the Alexandrinsky, the Bolshoi and the Maly! With this aim the new theater is to be established. The "Futurist."

6) Several presentations will be given in it (Moscow and Peter-City). Dramas to be put on: Kruchenykh's *Victory Over the Sun* (an opera), Mayakovsky's *Railroad,* Khlebnikov's *Christmas Story,* and others.

The wordcreators themselves, and the artists K. Malevich, D. Burliuk, and the musician M. Matiushin will direct the show.

Better to sweep away the old ruins and erect a sky-scraper as tenacious as a bullet![4]

The notice is signed by Kruchenykh and Malevich as "Chairman" and "Secretary," and dated 20 July 1913.

Back in Moscow after the summer "Congress," Malevich joined with Mayakovsky to seek to inaugurate the new theater under the auspices of The Union of Youth. Malevich wrote to Matiushin in Petersburg:

> . . . . Our Congress, with the main point about the theater in Moscow, has created great interest. The newspapers are all writing about it; today I had a correspondent from *The Morning of Russia (Utro Rossii);* of course he received all the necessary information. I think that in Petersburg the same thing will happen with the appearance of our activities. Mayakovsky and I have a suggestion for you, I hope that also Kruchenykh and you will join us. Namely, we are commissioning you to make a written application on behalf of all our theatrical work to the Union of Youth for backing us in the first show . . . .[5]

The Union of Youth had been interested for some time in extending its activity in the theater and so agreed to this proposal, undertaking the financial arrangements for *Victory Over the Sun,* and Mayakovsky's play, *Vladimir Mayakovsky.*

As Malevich had predicted, newspaper articles about the futurist works, rumors trickling out from the casting calls, and anticipation of a public scandal all generated a great deal of interest. The tickets were sold out in a day, in spite of the high price put on them by The "Union of Youth" in the hope of regaining its investment. Except for two professional singers in *Victory Over the Sun* (and Mayakovsky himself in *Vladimir Mayakovsky*) the performers in both works were amateurs, for the most part university students who had responded to a newspaper advertisement. *Victory Over the Sun* had to make do with just two rehearsals; the only music was provided by an old out-of-tune piano which had been dug up at the last moment. Performances took place from December 2-5, the two works alternating evenings. At the first night of *Victory Over the Sun*, the audience, packed into St. Petersburg's Luna Park Theater, was a variegated assembly—artists, journalists, army officers, members of the *duma*, and students—and its response was equally varied: boos, whistles, cheers, howls, and applause; the creators considered themselves a success.[6]

Victory Over the Sun is written in two "actions" *(dejmy)*, the first composed of four "scenes" *(kartiny)*, the second of two. The first part, sometimes indirectly, has to do with the capture of the sun, the second with the "tenth country" of the future after the sun has been subdued.

The text (published in 1914)[7] contains speech, songs, a scattering of simple stage directions, and a few lines of music. The cast includes two Futurist strongmen, a dusty traveler through time, an evil-intender, and a composite Nero-Caligula, the whining representative of the past. At first glance the opera appears to be chaotic. There is little development of character; in fact, the characters are really the one-dimensional personifications of qualities, found in morality plays. Their monologues are often completely unresponsive to one another, the "message" being directed primarily at the audience rather than at eliciting motivated action.[8] Kruchenykh uses neologisms, abbreviations, plays on words, and *zaum;* i.e., both groups of letters and individual letters which do not immediately convey logical meaning. At times the grammar is confused or ambiguous, but more frequently it is the illogicality of denotative meaning and imagery that is puzzling. Often both speech and action become patently absurd, but careful inspection reveals more than mere chaos. The effect is controlled, the madness methodical.

The central act of the opera, the capture of the sun, not only takes place offstage, but the audience sees very little activity overtly connected with this significant event. Instead, there is a series of vignettes which conveys the ambient violence and cool irrationality of the act. The first scene introduces most of the principal characters and establishes the intended conflict. The man-versus-sun image is archetypal of the futurist desire to transcend the merely present and visible. "The sun of cheap appearances,"[9] as Matiushin called it, is both the creator and symbol of visibility, and hence of things, of the illusion of reality; it is Apollo, the god of rationality and clarity, the light of logic, and hence the arch-enemy of all singers of the future. "We picked the sun with its fresh roots," the victors sing. "They're fatty, smelled of arithmetic."[10] The sun seduces man into an involvement with the present, feeds his passions and perpetuates his dependence on nature. In the sunless future there will be no such sentimentality:

> We don't have songs
> Of rewards of sighs
> That amused the mould
> Of rotten clothes! . . .
>
> Sun, you gave birth to passion
> And burned with an inflamed ray
> We will cover you with a dusty veil
> We will board you up in a concrete house![11]

Kruchenykh was not unique in his attitude toward the sun; in *Vladimir Mayakovsky, Victory's* co-production, the same sentiment is expressed:

> With swollen fingers in reddish hairs,
> the sun has caressed you with a gadfly's persistence:
> in your souls, a slave has been kissed to death.
> I, fearless,
> have born my hatred for daylight through centuries . . .[12]

In turning against the sun man turns on himself and his most obvious connection with the universe, violating his essential humanity for the purpose of transcending the limitations of his nature. The opera is drenched in violence, apparently unmotivated and unopposed. In the first scene, the evil-intender, a character defined by his name, shoots the traveler after speaking quite amicably to him, and intermittently carries on skirmishes with himself. A corpse who must be hidden helpfully drags itself off by the hair.

The second scene seems to take place during the fight with the sun. We see lame soldiers, again the evil-intender battles with himself, and the anti-aesthetic songs provide metaphoric images of the conflict:

> Start a fight with machine guns
> Crush them with a fingernail
> Then I will say: now you are
> Some strongmen!
>
> Let the scorching horses
> Stamp
> And the hair curl
> At the smell of skin! . . . .[13]

Scene 3 signals the end of the conflict. It consists of only one song, that of the gravediggers, which lists images of death:

Smash a turtle
Fall upon the cradle
Of a bloodthirsty turnip
Welcome the cage

A fat bedbug smells of the grave . . .
A black leg . . .
The crushed coffin rocks
Curls the lace of shavings.[14]

In the fourth and last scene of Act 1, news of the sun's capture is relayed by a speaker on the telephone: "What? They've seized the sun? Thank you."[15] The scene concludes with a vision of the new age by the new people:

The sun of iron age is dead! The cannons are shattered
ratchets and wheels drop like wax before our gaze! . . .

−To more massive steps
Forged not from fire
Not of iron and marble
Not of air stoves
  In smoke carbon monoxide
  And thick dust
  The blows get stronger
  We grow healthy like pigs
  We are dark in appearance
  Our insides are light
  The sickly udder of the red dawn
  Warms us
  BRN BRN[16]

The new age has arrived in the second act. Both scenes take place in the "tenth country" in a restricted, house-like structure. The past has been shot, we are told in the first scene, and is gone, and with it went memories and mistakes and the bending of knees: "You become like a clean mirror or a fish reservoir where in a clear grotto carefree golden fish wag their tails like thankful turks."[17] And yet things are not perfect. As was predicted in the first act, "there is no happiness there everyone looks happy and immortal."[18] Now "it has become easy for everyone to breathe and many people don't know what to do with themselves for the great lightness. Several tried to drown themselves, the weak ones went out of their minds, saying: we can really become terrible and strong. It oppressed them."[19] A fat man who had been asleep wakes up bewildered and asks, "where is the sunset?" while a skull gallops about on four legs.

The last scene of the opera opens with the fat man imprisoned in the house.

> The tenth country . . . the windows are all constructed
> inside the house is fenced in you live here as you
> know well the 10th countries. And here I didn't
> know one must stay locked up.[20]

He climbs up into the "brain" of the house, tries in vain to set his watch and stares disconsolately out the window:

> yes yes perhaps see yesterday here there was a telegraph
> pole and today there is a buffet well and tomorrow
> there will probably be bricks
> daily this happens with us no one knows where the
> stop is and where they will have dinner[21]

At the sound of a propeller, a young man runs in and sings a "frightened vulgar song" which begins with nine lines of individual sounds and develops into a series of surreal images. Sportsmen enter:

> here . . . everything runs without
> resistance
> here paths make their way from all sides
> they engine a hundred hooves
> they outrun they trick the clumsy
>   they simply squeeze
>   be careful of motley-eyed
>   monsters . . .
> futurists countries will exist
> if these wires bother anyone he can turn his back[22]

They sing a song which develops into meaningless sounds and is interrupted by an airplane falling onto the stage. The dialogue continues in *zaum* phrases. The aviator appears unharmed and sings a "military song" of individual sounds. The opera ends with the same thought with which it began:

> All's well that
> begins well
>   and has no end
> the world will perish but we have no
>   end![23]

All in all, a rather remarkable picture of the future emerges from *Victory Over the Sun.* Although the future-land is not specifically located in time or space, it is clearly not on the earth as we know it, or dependent on earthly considerations. A universalism projects the opera beyond conventional human values, so that good and bad seem no longer to apply. We are left with an ambivalent feeling about the new age, uncertain whether to welcome or dread its approach. Only one thing is certain: the Futurists' commitment to the future, *no matter what it may be.* The only definitive, positive qualities of the new men are physical health and strength which seem to flow from an inexhaustible inner source. There are no memories, no dreams, no love, indeed no sentiment at all; even violence is passionless, a kind of mickey-mouse cruelty without purpose. It is a confining environment, uncomfortable, with little movement permitted and no way out. Even the windows are "inside." A sad fatalism hangs over the whole vision. We *know* that the unreconstructed fat man is grasping at straws when he thinks of fighting back: "Cannons out of birch—think!"[24] Nothing will come of it.

The similarities in form and content between *Victory Over the Sun* and *Vladimir Mayakovsky* are striking. Both works are written in two acts and are set in an indefinite time and place, except that the second act of each takes place in a projected future. The characters in *Vladimir Mayakovsky,* as in *Victory Over the Sun,* have no proper names or distinct personalities and are not meant to be believable human beings. Neither work has the usual dramatic structure and in fact there is very little plot at all. Even though actors enter and leave the stage, and things "happen," the action has neither motivation nor effect and hence makes no logical progress. Although Kruchenykh's and Mayakovsky's literary styles differ, both place the emphasis of the work on imagery and the poetic treatment of language, rather than on the development of a narrative or dramatic structure.

Several themes are common to the two works: the revelation of "new souls," the destruction of the world, and an inclination to violence and death. But most interesting is the similarity of the two visions of the future. In *Vladimir Mayakovsky,* the poet's enslavement in spite of being king of the future, his crushing burden of grief, and the loss of free will, serve to produce the same sort of final ambiguity found in *Victory Over the Sun.* We also have the same synthesis of anti-sentimentalism and sadness. "They say that somewhere—in Brazil, I think, there is one happy man!" the poet sighs, and "I may be the last poet."[25] Another character, the man with one ear, feels the same way: "My own sorrow grows—it is inexplicable and alarming," he cries.[26] As its subtitle indicates, *Vladimir Mayakovsky* is a tragedy, and so is *Victory Over the Sun;* in spite of their laughter and absurdities, both works are ultimately depressing. Mayakovsky later gave more complete expression to this theme in *The Bedbug,* but oddly, even in 1913 the Futurists darkly glimpsed the future.

The style of *Victory Over the Sun* reflects this picture of the future. The language is strong, unyielding (a quality Kruchenykh tried to enhance by having each syllable spoken slowly and separately) and at times even feminine word endings are dropped. Often the grammar skids crazily beyond logic to puzzle and imprison tidy minds like the sun in its concrete maze. Nor is there an escape on an orderly sequence of images. There seem to be no causal relationships to grasp hold of, no point toward which anything leads. The text is cooly absurd, a disengaged inanity that takes a curious sensual pleasure in the jingle of words, the play of cardboard violence, the refusal of rationality. It is the prattling idiocy induced by certain horror and no exit. The imagination runs loose, automatically associating one word with the next without regard for sense. Catachresis is based on similarities of sound; for example, *"vot by"* instead of *"khot' by"* or *"makhaet rozami"* for *"makhaet rukami."*[27] Illogical associations are conjured up by the familiarity of common phrases:

> The speed you see is expressed if times two root
> teeth one put a coach of old boxes and sprinkles
> them with yellow sand yes and so let all
> that when you yourself think Well in the simplest
> case they collide into some thathere pipe
> in an easy chair well but if not? See there the
> people all climbed up somewhere s'high that
> its not his business hw the engines feel there
> their hoofs and all well its natural![28]

The language also twists beneath the pressure of strong emotion. Behind the meaning of a new phrase the memory of the old one may lurk, a shadow of rhythm and sound. "All hands on deck!" *"Saryn' na kichku!"* the evil-intender calls desperately, only it comes out *"kichku v kapuste!"* "Decks in the cabbage!" The galloping emotion bursts out in new images, as fresh and beyond logic as emotion and the situation itself. Kruchenykh's language is thus expressive rather than communicative in the usual sense—poetic, abstract, almost devoid of narrative content. The chaotic blossoming of absurd, sometimes surreal, images is only incidentally an effort to scandalize the bourgeoisie. More importantly, it is an attempt to shock everyone, even the Futurists themselves, into a new consciousness. *Victory Over the Sun* swamped the senses and saturated the intellect with irreducible objects in order to stimulate the viewer to another level of intuitive and emotional understanding of reality. "Dissonance," Kruchenykh said, is a mirror of the "soul"; imagination unencumbered by patterned causal thinking and buoyed by a feeling of silly superhuman strength perceives a reality unobtainable by reason, an internal reality, which, being inherently closer to "truth," generates the "sensation" of our future existence. Kruchenykh conceived of his "beyond mind" language as a language which is produced as an automatic reflex and directly communicates internal states; it is communicative by virtue of originating out of a shared humanity. Such a language, in turn, alters perception and gives visions of the approaching world. Its possibilities and the circumstances in which it is actualized are explored by *Victory Over the Sun*. The *zaum* in the opera is clearly intended to be the language of the future, but it is interesting also that it is usually fear which triggers a character's transition from absurd speech to *zaum*. Perhaps

Kruchenykh came by default to fear as the only emotion strong enough to touch off *zaum;* love and hence, presumably, hate do not exist in his future.

Malevich's sketches for the costumes for *Victory Over the Sun*[29] show that for all the characters he planned costumes based on geometrical shapes, sometimes with added abstract designs. The bully wears a short triangular "skirt," the strong man is composed completely of triangles, the legs of the attentive worker are built of doughnut-shaped rings. The costumes seem to have been a deliberate attempt to reproduce on the stage the simplified geometric figures of Malevich's paintings of this time, for example those in *The Woodcutter* or *Morning in the Village After Snowfall.* Kruchenykh suggested this when, in the first half of October 1913, he wrote to Matiushin: "I have been thinking privately about the play and it seems to me that it would be good, perhaps, if the actors were similar to the figure on the cover of *The Three (Troe)* and spoke coarsely and low . . ." There are very few precise descriptions of Malevich's sets or costumes as they actually appeared at the performance, and only two contemporary photographs have so far been published. In 1914 Matiushin stated that the costumes were not made according to the drawings, but we do know that there were costumes made of cardboard which looked vaguely like armor, and that actors wore masks.[30] This seems to suggest that the costumes were at least something like the drawings. In his memoirs, Matiushin noted that the strongmen were made to seem gigantic: the shoulders of their costumes were at the height of the actor's mouths and their huge cardboard heads towered above them. We may also assume from contemporary remarks, and from the fact that Malevich himself painted the sets, that they were of the same general design as his preparatory sketches.

These sketches show a square-shaped area with a smaller square centered within it. The corners of the two squares are joined by diagonal lines so as to give the impression of inwardly slanting sides. The viewer seems to "look out" from inside a box. We may suppose that this format represents a standard "box set," whose sides were flats and whose central, inner square was the backdrop. Onto this basic form Malevich projected both linear and cubist drawings in which one may recognize objects referred to in the libretto. Beneath the sketches are (sometimes ambiguous) notes designating the scenes for which the design is intended. There are sketches for Act I, Scenes 2 and 3, and for the house of the second act. There is also the famous "abstract" backdrop which is designated for Act I, Scene 1, and for Act II, Scene 1. On the cover of the published opera is another sketch, also based on the square-within-a-square format. Its central square contains a stylized sun, along with part of an airplane, an oversized comma, and a large "KP," presumably the beginning of Kruchenykh's name in Cyrillic. The sides of the box are decorated with references to the sky, as well as with other unidentifiable shapes and shadows. Benedikt Livshits, who was present at the first performance of *Victory Over the Sun,* reproduces in his memoirs a drawing by Malevich which he says is connected with *Victory Over the Sun.*[31] Although it is flat and not done in the box-set format it does incorporate words and portions of words, written and printed, which refer to the sun and planets.

Livshits describes two additional elements in Malevich's decor. The first was the presence onstage of either painted representations or actual volumetric freestanding shapes which seem to have been arranged according to size. The second, perhaps more striking, element is the use of mobile lighting to articulate disembodied shapes and movements:

> Out of the primal night the tentacles of the projectors snatched part of first one and then another object and, saturating it with color, brought it to life. It was not even comparable to the "fairy lamp effects" which were in use in theaters of the time. The innovation and originality of Malevich's device consisted first of all in the use of light as a principle which creates form, which legitimizes the existence of a thing in space . . . .
>
> Within the limits of the stage box a painted solid geometry came into being for the first time, a strict system of volumes, reducing to a minimum the elements of chance which are thrust on it from without by the movements of the human figures. The figures themselves were sliced by the blades of the beams; alternately hands, feet, head, were eliminated, since for Malevich they were only geometrical bodies subject not only to decomposition into component parts, but also to complete dissolution in pictorial space . . . . Instead of the square, instead of the circle, toward which Malevich was already trying to bring his painting, he had the possibility of using them as their volumetric correlatives, the cube and the sphere.[32]

The fact that all the forms onstage—the geometric shapes,[33] the costumes—can be found in Malevich's backdrops is striking. Apparently his intention was to make the flat backdrops look three-dimensional—not only recessive but also as if, in the fragmenting light, parts of them also projected forward, to mingle with the similar shapes of the costumes and volumes. In addition, the moving figures of the actors and the roving spotlights from the projectors situated, perhaps, on opposite sides of the theater, animated the entire stage so that the composition was subject to continuous variation. Kruchenykh, who was also the director of the opera, mentioned the importance of movement in it:

> They [the costumes] transformed the human anatomy and the actors moved, held and [were] directed by the rhythm dictated by the artist and director.[34]

The ambiguity of the spatial relationships, especially in the perception of depth, undoubtedly was increased by the "tunnel effect" created by the receding centers of the backdrops. The center back plane seems, from the sketches, to open into infinity, which greatly elongated the axis of depth. This effect can be visualized quite clearly, for example, in the design which appeared on the cover of the libretto. The section of an airplane occupies the entire height of the extreme left, with the large schematic sun just behind it. On the right, the huge initials and comma hang in the air, their positions relative to the rest of the pictorial space unclearly defined. Below the letters, converging lines lead the eye back into emptiness. The viewer, while confined by the sides of the "box," faces an opening into endless space. The backdrop for a house for the last scene of the opera works in a similar way. The sides and bottom of the "box" are left relatively free of structure. The house itself is located entirely within the back square (which here is larger than that in the other sketches) except at the top where the massive forms extend to the stage ceiling, i.e., to the limit of the outer square. Thus the house is located slightly forward of the usual very distant plane, just within the "box." In spite of this, and the fact that this design appears more dense and impenetrable than the others, there is an opening into deeper space. Just above the center of the picture an exact square is outlined, empty except for a rectangular grid in its upper lefthand corner and a circular "clock" in the upper right. Apparently, it is the interior of the house which is pictured here, and the small empty square is the window through which the fat man looks out at the tower clock and eventually exits.

The supposedly abstract design is marked Act I, Scene 1, and Act II, Scene 1 (a designation for Scene 2 has been crossed out). It is of the same square-within-a-square design, and it is reasonable to suppose that only the central square was a backdrop and that it too was intended to make reference to the imagery of the opera. Although at first glance the inner square seems to be divided by a diagonal into a black and a white triangle, this in fact is not the case. The dividing line between black and white is actually curved downward slightly so that it intersects the small square on its lower edge, about a tenth of the way in along the total width of the square. Thus the inner square may well be meant to show a small section of an enormous sun. Since the sun is the dominant motif of the opera, its looming presence in the first scene of each act, its great hulk made larger by the inability to contain all of it in our field of view, is plausible. The partial view of the sun gives us a position relative to it unlike our actual one: an ambiguous proximity which suggests either that the sun has been confined closer to us on earth, or that we have moved out into space. The sensation of being without bounds, of free flight, is, of course, one of Malevich's favorite metaphors for Suprematism. The ambiguity here also parallels the ambiguous nature of the opera's projected future. From a formal standpoint, a representational reading of the drawing is not inconsistent with Malevich's strong interest in sections of curved planes confined within rectangular planes. Examples may be found in *The Guardsman* (1913) and *Musical Instrument/Lamp* (1913)[35] and of course in the set design which appears on the libretto cover. Both the interest in form and dynamics and the specifically planetary references come together in a later series of analytical Suprematist drawings. The drawing *Suprematis* (1914, 1917), for example, bears the note "passage of the Supreme along the surface of a white disk." The disk is indicated by a single curved line extending from the top of the picture almost to the bottom. In a note to a drawing which is filled with inscribed arcs, Malevich says that it is necessary to determine which arc "will give . . . the greatest expression of dynamic and spatial sensation," and that the arcs are a "search for the legitimate establishment of a sphere or a rounded surface."[36] Spheres in these drawings are not only given by a single line. In *Study Suprematis 52 System A4* (ca. 1918), the lower left hand corner of the rectangular limits of the drawing is occupied by a section of a pink disk against a white field, a composition especially reminiscent of the backdrop sketch for *Victory Over the Sun.*

Thus it may be argued that Malevich did not intend this backdrop to be abstract in the usual sense, and that it was in the search for a transcendent psychological sensation without conventional reference to the everyday world—a visual analogue to *zaum*—that he hit upon a close-up view of this large, simple and symbolic object. It is undoubtedly true that other elements in the opera's decor were purely geometric: the painted volumes and the costumes. But in these cases too, the geometric shapes may have been intended to function as *portions* of the background scenery which consisted mainly of stylized and schematized references to things.

The forms in Malevich's Suprematist pictures, though they come to function as autonomous and abstract units, derive from cohesive and recognizable objects. And the spatial relationships of these units are those of individual objects to one another; only their specific identities have been subtracted (though these sometimes reappear in the titles). For this reason, Suprematism was, as Malevich called it, "the new realism"—an elicitation of the more genuine reality of the future.[37]

The dynamism of the Suprematist style, especially evident in later, more complex examples, has a possible antecedent in Malevich's conception of a continuously mobile decor for *Victory Over the Sun.* The opera's light-fragmented spectacle of movement in real time and space may well have augmented the artist's impulse to impart a dynamic sense to his abstract pictures, by arranging their pictorial elements to spark the same kind of sensation of space, timelessness and new reality for which the opera strove.

But the most specific link between Malevich's decor and his new style is the square-within-a-square format that represents the box-set. Its focal squares at the back of enclosed framing space will give birth to Malevich's "royal infant," the *Square.* The emotional impact he attributed to the square—empty of objects but full of sensation, a window in the visible universe looking into a new reality—corresponds strikingly to its original function in the theater. There seems to be no reason to doubt that 1914 was indeed "the year when the square appeared." The "abstract" sun design was halfway to its realization. All that remained was to eliminate the four diagonal lines that represented the third dimension of the box set.

Suprematism thus followed logically from the puzzles and proliferation of objects in the alogist paintings; both the intention and treatment of elements were similar. Malevich even made a brief attempt to combine individual Suprematist elements with realistic line drawings. A series of undated drawings from a private collection in the Soviet Union shows arrangements of Suprematist rectangles and, among other things, fish, a playing card, a shovel, and a boat.[38] Hardest of all for Malevich was to abandon the human figure which consistently had been the primary image and psychological subject of his work. One of this same series of drawings is a man composed of rectangles, and in at least two later Suprematist paintings,[39] the geometric elements echo the ghostly figure of a man.

Malevich, Bergson, and the Italian Futurists: 1914-1915

It is readily evident from press reports of the Cubo-Futurists' activities and from Kruchenykh's technical and polemical writings of 1913 that the course of the Italian Futurist movement was well known to the Russians at that time and that they felt free to adapt its notions for their own interpretation of the new art. But although the Russians did not sympathize with every aspect of Italian Futurism—they felt particularly uncertain about Marinetti's glorification of physical violence and war, and did not make such direct connections between politics and literature—they did not begin to be particularly anxious about being associated with their Italian counterparts until late in 1913 when Russian critics began to question the Cubo-Futurists' originality. Kruchenykh made derogatory remarks about the Italians in *The Three,* published in September. In November, about a month before the performances of *Victory Over the Sun* and *Vladimir Mayakovsky,* the Burliuks, Mayakovsky, Khlebnikov, and Kamensky appeared at the Polytechnical Museum in Moscow for an evening devoted to "An Affirmation of Russian Futurism." In his presentation, "The Achievements of Futurism," Mayakovsky, particularly, denied that Russian Futurism was an "imitation" of Marinetti, proclaimed its prior origin and its independence, and condemned the Italians for their bellicosity.[1] Rumors of the Russian attitude reached Marinetti, just then planning his first (and only) trip to Russia,[2] and he responded furiously in a letter to *The Russian Gazette (Russkie Vedomosti):*

> There can be no argument that the word Futurism (Futurists, Futuristic) appeared in Russia after my first manifesto was printed in "Figaro" and reprinted by the most important newspapers throughout the world and, of course, by Russian newspapers and journals.[3]

Marinetti was certainly right about Russian artists' awareness of Italian Futurism from its beginning in 1909; but as we have seen, for several years after that the Russians were preoccupied with other interests, and more recently, they felt they had gone considerably beyond Marinetti's theories. To make matters worse, Marinetti's invitation to visit Russia had had nothing to do with the Russian Futurists. It had been extended by Genrikh Tasteven, an editor of the then defunct *Golden Fleece,* who had met Marinetti in Paris.[4] But although the Cubo-Futurists were not especially anxious to admit a debt to Marinetti, most of the avant-garde, including Malevich, Kulbin and Matiushin, were at least determined to be polite when he arrived. Only the usually gentle Velimir Khlebnikov and normally difficult Mikhail Larionov were especially hostile. Khlebnikov tried to distribute bitterly worded leaflets at one of Marinetti's Petersburg lectures, and Larionov recommended throwing rotten eggs.[5]

The high emotion and defensiveness excited by the appearance of Marinetti at the beginning of 1914 might be construed as a Russian effort to conceal what they felt to be damning evidence of Italian influence, and indeed, some of the literary Futurists did try to obscure the dates of some of their early publications. But it is also important to remember that the Italian painting manifestos and the full impact of Futurist painting itself appeared somewhat later than Marinetti's first literary manifesto of 1909; so that it is quite certain that whatever their effect had on Russian painting, it was superimposed on the lively interest in the new theories and painting from France and Germany which we have already noted.[6]

Furthermore, as we have also seen, Kruchenykh's literary doctrine contained a strong strain of the absurd based partly on the belief that "art goes in the vanguard of psychic evolution"; thus the new sensibility claimed by the Cubo-Futurists was a result not of the artifacts of modern living, as Marinetti suggested, but rather of a change in human consciousness so radical that for all intents and purposes it removed its possessor from this earth. (Larionov, too, had spoken quite disparagingly of the earth in his manifesto of December 1913, and this was one notion that he shared with others of his fellow modernists.) The literary theories of Kruchenykh had philosophical implications far in excess of Marinetti's free-floating adjectives or the destruction of syntax for the sake of condensed metaphors. The strong emotion responsible for the destruction of syntax was associated for the Italian with "wars and shipwrecks";[7] for the Russians it was induced by their first glimpse of the living universe. *Zaum,* as it was expounded by Kruchenykh, was not based on a disordered urban "madness," but was rather a constructive principle by which one might achieve insights into an ontological, if fearsome, reality.

After Larionov's break with Kruchenykh because of his association with the *Union of Youth,* Malevich became Kruchenykh's principal illustrator.[8] Some of his drawings of this period were closely related to Italian Futurist work and were the experiments which provided Malevich with essential concepts and the visual vocabulary for an eventual entry into abstraction. Of the Futurist work available to him at the time, probably the formal and cubist oriented work of Severini was most attractive. Echoes of Severini's work may be found throughout Malevich's painting of this period; we will point out just a few. Although the stylistic method of *Morning in the Village After the Snowfall* is not completely analogous to Severini's *The Boulevard,* the patterned geometricism which unifies figures and landscape, the repeated planar hills, the treatment of light and shadow, and Malevich's sudden reliance on the straight line suggest that Malevich may have seen this work. Perhaps it was in the process of adapting his peasant figures to the requirements of this picture (the motifs are similar to Goncharova's *Skating Scene,* 1908) that Malevich arrived at the rigorously geometric figures which are found in his work beginning about the same time. Intermediate stages in the development of this figure may be seen in *Peasant Woman with Buckets and Child* and *Taking in the Rye,* both exhibited slightly earlier. Malevich had had an opportunity to use such figures in actual motion in *Victory Over the Sun,* when he had projected light onto individual portions of the costumes and scenery to produce a faceted effect, suggested perhaps by Severini's series of paintings of dancers.[9] During the year Malevich published drawings of a woman reaping in which the dynamism outward from the center of the figure and the rhythmic arcs defining its periphery are reminiscent of works such as *The Bear's Dance* and *Dancer at Pigal's.* For *Victory* Malevich envisioned the unattached geometrical shapes of the sort found in Severini's *Yellow Dancer,* where the geometrical forms apparently float freely in the air like sparkles in a beam of light.[10] There is also an interesting parallel between Severini's objectless *From Nothing to the Real* and the proto-Suprematist drawing by Malevich which appeared in *The Three.* In addition to the similarities in the abstract forms, Severini's title exactly expresses the role that Malevich's experiments with light played in the evolution of Suprematism.

Like the Italian Futurists, Malevich made use of Bergsonian concepts concerning the nature of memory and the mutual interaction of object and environment. Remembered visual impressions such as may be found in Severini's *Memories of a Journey* appear in *Englishman in Moscow.* Fragmented impressions of activity on the street are combined in the preparatory sketch for *Woman at a Tram Stop,* a drawing which is similar in its accumulation of objects to Boccioni's study for *Horizontal Construction.* The final versions of these works, however, are extremely different. While Boccioni eventually integrated the central figure and environment through a cubist reworking of both, Malevich retained the realistically drawn and apparently unrelated "remembered" objects, and embedded them in a cubist environment. The "woman," as the thinking subject, is suppressed, destroying the logical link between objects, and resulting in a perfect example of *zaum.*

In June and July 1913, almost two years before the first Suprematist pictures were begun, Malevich wrote two letters to Matiushin in which he discussed the newly invented *zaum* style in literature and in painting. He said:

I think that:
1) Art is that which not everyone can penetrate in a thing, and what is left over is only for the monsters of time.
2) That one must not draw even one line without the control of reason and sense, and among us one finds most of all works done in some kind of compulsive, senseless cramp.

We have come as far as the rejection of reason, but we rejected reason because another kind of reason has grown in us, which in comparison to what we have rejected, can be called 'beyond reason,' [*zaumnyi*] which also has law, construction [*konstruktsiia*], and sense, and only by learning it shall we have work based on the law of the truly new 'beyond reason.' This reason has found Cubism as a means of expressing a thing.

We have arrived at beyond-reason-ness. I don't know whether you agree with me or not, but I am beginning to understand that in this beyond-reason there is also a strict law which gives pictures their right to exist. And not one line should be drawn without the consciousness of its law, then only are we alive.[11]

These letters point up very clearly what often tends to be forgotten about *zaum*—and, as we shall see, about Suprematism—that it did have "sense," that there was a perceived structure, and that it was not all emotional or anti-intellectual. *Zaum*, and Suprematism, which was to derive directly from it, had as its primary object the widening of the possibilities of analytical logic; it appealed to the totality of the psyche, but with the understanding that the psyche, too, obeys a natural law, as does every other thing in nature. And in working with as broad a range as possible of human experiences, Malevich and others hoped to discover new laws, new principles, with which they might create a broad new art. The popular reasoning went as follows: our logic, as was pointed out by Darwin and many others, is a product of evolutionary experience; it developed in order to cope with situations which were important to the preservation of the species. This sort of reason, as Malevich was fond of saying, is therefore purely "utilitarian." It is only part of man's potential. But art should not be a product of this partial reason, rather it should make use of the whole of the psyche, its vitality, its capacity for novelty and for true creation. As we have seen, the Cubo-Futurists used in their work chance, the absurd, the ugly and the anti-aesthetic because they believed all these things a part of a natural, lawful reality, and they had as their goal the depiction of all of that reality.

It is possible to give a general description of the universe, the transcendent reality, as envisaged by Malevich and his friends in the period of 1914-1915. It was essentially the popular turn-of-the-century view. Vaguely uneasy with the strictly mechanical, Newtonian universe, they had not yet fully assimilated the revolutionary work of Minkowski or Einstein and so were inclined to a "cosmic dynamism," bolstered by ideas borrowed from Bergson, whom they were in the process of reading. The universe was both material and immaterial, thus it was difficult to visualize or describe precisely. Matter and energy were related, and space and time could no longer be considered separately. The universe was extremely large. Perhaps because of flying, the newly popular sport, everyone was suddenly aware of a cosmos of immense proportions; the earth, a tiny round planet, seemed a currant buried somewhere in an enormous cosmic cake. And the whole was continually in motion, not with the tidy circularities of Newton's orbits, but with a kind of superfluidity of waves, oscillations, vibrations, and currents. Such a universe no longer seemed quite predictable, an idea which was also confirmed by Bergson. The Cubo-Futurists were inclined to think of the world's form and motion as organic, i.e., its motion was visualized as a moving away from a center or centers, an opening out, its forms multiplying and in general behaving in the complex and creative way associated with organic life. The role of the individual person in such a universe is merely to participate in the ongoing development, i.e., to cultivate his own evolution. The artist, assumed to be slightly ahead of others in this process, had the responsibility to perceive more fully and to interpret his vision for the rest of society.

These general background ideas allow us to consider Malevich's initial approach to Suprematism, the most basic elements of which appear to have been formulated between November 1914 and May 1915.[12] Fundamentally, Malevich proposed a revolution of consciousness, a change in what he called the old "habits of mind." Depicting the visible form of objects gets the artist nowhere, he said, no matter what he does with them. From his Alogist experiments and from Cubism, Malevich had concluded that there were endless things and endless ways to depict them, and none brings one any closer to the true nature of reality. As long as representational forms are used, any progress toward a greater truth is an illusion—there are always more objects over the next hill—and *objects tie the mind to the limited form of reason.* That is why he eventually concluded that Cubo-Futurism did not work; the mind got bogged down with objects and failed to make the leap to the greater reality. Malevich's proposition, then, was that before he applied paint to canvas, the artist *himself* undergoes that alteration of consciousness which previously had been left to the viewer, thus allowing true perception to become explicit on the canvas once again.

The artist, therefore, should first change himself, especially his old habit of seeing "things." The process is particularly difficult because the body itself is one of the "things" of this earth. Malevich suggested two ways to escape, or at least to attenuate, one's physical self: to develop the inner consciousness and to avoid spatial relationships with other objects, i.e., to remove oneself from the earth. In a letter to Matiushin shortly after the first exhibition of his Suprematist works, Malevich pointed out this relationship between space and objects:

> The keys of Suprematism lead me to the discovery of the still unrealized. My new painting does not belong to the earth exclusively. The earth is thrown away like a house eaten up by termites. And, in fact, in man, in his consciousness, there lies a striving towards space, the pull of a "take-off" from the earth.
> [In] Futurism, in Cubism, space, almost exclusively, is cultivated, but its form, being connected with objectness, does not convey even to the imagination the

> presence of world space; its space is limited to the space shared by things on the earth.
>
> The hung plane of painted color on a white canvas sheet gives a strong sensation of space directly to our consciousness. I am transported into endless emptiness, where you sense around you the creative points of the universe.[13]

This leaving of the earth, at least the earth as we know it, i.e., the removal of recognizable objects and the cultivation of an indefinite spatial locus, was first used by Malevich in the "Sun" backdrop for *Victory Over the Sun*. It is a device calculated to deny the viewer a sense of his own form or size while encouraging the mind to remain open.

The inner consciousness Malevich called "intuition." Some care must be taken with this term. Malevich did not advocate intuition as a kind of passive, anti-intellectual approach to art. It is definitely not instinct. He advanced intuition as an active creative principle which is lawful; in this it was quite similar to the original principle of *zaum*. For while it rejects analytical logic alone as too limiting, it certainly includes analytical logic and demands of the intellect the greatest effort. Indeed, Malevich often called this intuition "intuitive reason" or "intuitive will." Intuitive reason may be unconscious, but it should not be. The artist must work to become distinctly conscious of his intuition so that its forms can be revealed clearly on the canvas.

> The artist should now know what, and why, things happen in his pictures.
> Formerly he lived by some kind of mood. He awaited the rising of the moon, twilight, put green shades on his lamps, and this all tuned his mood like a violin.
> But when asked why this face was crooked, or green, he could not give an exact answer.
> "I want it so, I like it like that . . . ."
> . . . . .
> Being a painter, I ought to say why in pictures people's faces are painted green and red.[14]

Malevich believed that intuition becomes gradually more conscious in the course of evolution and the effect of this is to create a new vision. Thus we see the objects in painting undergoing greater and greater distortions. When art becomes completely non-utilitarian, i.e., out of the grasp of the old, purely utilitarian logic, the painter will no longer have to look to objects for his forms. The intuition itself will create them. "The forms of Suprematism," Malevich wrote, "are already proof of the construction of forms from nothing, discovered by Intuitive Reason."[15] This is as close to true creation as one can get. The bringing forth of something out of nothing. "The square is not a subconscious form," Malevich tells us. "The Square is a Living Royal Infant."[16]

Malevich's insistence that new forms be elicited by intuition was ultimately the basis of his criticism of Italian Futurism. Although he agreed with its intention to depict the impression of movement, he found its ability to convey reality limited by the use of naturalistic, even though fragmented, objects.

> The conglomeration of objects is received not from intuitive sense, but from a purely visual impression, while the design, the construction of the picture, is calculated to achieve an impression. . . .
> Consequently we have nothing purely intuitive in the picture.[17]

Malevich criticized the Futurists on their own ground, for it was they, rather than Malevich, who originally introduced the term "intuition" into Futurist theory. Umberto Boccioni, particularly, adapted it from Henri Bergson, and several of Malevich's ideas may be usefully compared with those of Bergson. Although Bergson is not explicitly mentioned by name in Malevich's writings, his concepts are present throughout, at times very clearly. It is not surprising that this should be so. Bergson was enjoying great popularity at this time, even in Russia. By the middle of 1914 every major work of Bergson had been translated into Russian, including *Introduction to Metaphysics, Matter and Memory, Creative Evolution* and *Time and Free Will,* and during 1913 and 1914 a five volume "collected works" was published.[18] Moreover, the Italian Futurists had applied Bergson's discussion of intuition and analysis, time and duration to their own painting and theories, and Malevich knew these very well. As we have noted, from the middle of 1912 interest in the Italian work had been intense among the Russian avant-garde. Boccioni's important introduction to the Paris Exhibition catalogue had been reproduced in Russian by the *Union of Youth* journal as early as June 1912, and later the connection between Futurism and Bergson had been made all too concrete in such articles as I. Rozenfeld's "Intuitivism and Futurism."[19] After Marinetti's visit to Russia in January 1914, all the major manifestos were reprinted in Russian.[20] Nikolai Kulbin had attempted to question Marinetti about Bergson while Marinetti was in St. Petersburg, but Marinetti was quick to assert that Bergson was of no relevance and to complain that every time the word intuition was mentioned people leapt to Bergson's name.[21]

While at the time this was undoubtedly true—and Marinetti had less to do with Bergson than Boccioni—it would be hard to conclude that Malevich's intuition derived from any other source. Like Malevich's creative principle, Bergson's intuition was a deliberate and intellectual attempt to change the old habits of mind. Bergson called it "intellectual sympathy" and "intellectual auscultation," and pointed to its "essentially active, I might almost say violent character." It was characteristic of Bergson's, as well as Malevich's, intuition that it be consistent with scientific or analytical knowledge, nor did it appeal necessarily to the subconscious.

> In order to reach intuition it is not necessary to transport ourselves outside the domain of the senses and of consciousness . . . I recommend a certain manner of thinking which courts difficulty; I value effort above everything.

> The mind has to do violence to itself, has to reverse the direction of the operation by which it habitually thinks.[22]

Malevich often echoed Bergson when he spoke of the "inner struggle" between the two modes of reason. Bergson's emphasis on the fact that intuition functioned to make vague or unclear perceptions more clearly conscious and focused, promoting a wider field of understanding, is also precisely the interpretation given to it by Malevich.

But however appealing Bergson's intuition may have been for the Suprematists, there was one important problem for them in Bergsonian concepts: Bergson maintained that the reason analytical thought was so poorly adapted to perceiving the true nature of reality was the habit of visualization, the habit of thinking with, as Bergson called it, "the logic of solid bodies," which had been bred into the species over long years of evolution and which was now limiting the capacity to grasp fundamental concepts of space and time. According to Bergson, if the universe is to be understood, it must be without an image because reality is essentially non-pictorial. Images only work in the very limited middle strata of nature, the earthly dimensions between atoms and the cosmos that have been useful for practical purposes. An image of an object always represents a symbolic view, it is stable, whereas reality is not stable; an image necessitates a point of view outside, whereas intuition understands from within.

Obviously, such an idea would be problematical for any painter; Boccioni had difficulties with it, but it was especially troublesome for Malevich because his ambitions had never fallen within the middle strata, the purely earthly realm. In fact, the main thrust of Malevich's vision as a painter had been toward the opposite extremes: the personal consciousness and the cosmic environment. Bergson had stated precisely the problem Malevich encountered with *zaum*. The old logic was inescapably tied to pictorialization, and for a painter it was hard to know where to turn to escape it. From Bergson it was at least obvious that to avoid the "three dimensional logic" and the "law of causality" one had to move away from the middle strata to the extremes. To avoid representation of definable distances, points of view and the relationships of things, earthly form itself must be abandoned; only by removing one's physical self can one escape from the "beloved objects and little corners of nature."[23] The problem thus became the extinction of the external self; Bergson, in another connection, provides a description of this process:

> I am going to close my eyes, stop my ears, extinguish one by one the sensations that come to me from the outer world. Now it is done; all my perceptions vanish, the material universe sinks into silence and the night. I subsist, however, and cannot help myself subsisting, I am still there, with the organized sensations which come to me from the surface and from the interior of my body, with the recollections which my past perceptions have left behind them—nay, with the impression, most positive and full, of the void I have just made about me . . .
> When I no longer know anything of external objects, it is because I have taken refuge in the consciousness that I have of my self . . . .
> I can by turns imagine a nought of external perception or a nought of internal

perception . . . the absence of one consists, at bottom, in the exclusive presence of the other.[24]

The intuitive knowledge of psychological existence is essentially inner, without any imaginable form, and it is this inner knowledge—of a variety of qualities and continuous flux—which is the key to the real external world.

> There is a reality that is external and yet given immediately to the mind . . . The consciousness we have of our own self in its continual flux introduces us to the interior of a reality, on the model of which we must represent other realities.[25]

The triumphant sound of success at this intensely difficult psychological alteration rings in Malevich's declaration at the first display of his Suprematist work:

> I have transformed myself into the zero of form and dragged myself out of Academic Art's whirlpool of trash.
> I have wiped out the ring of the horizon and gotten out of the circle of things. . . .[26]

The reduction of external self and object to zero, the rejection of form and a beginning with the void, was a fundamental premise of Suprematism. In the 1920's Malevich and his followers tried again to make this very specific in their statement about the Suprematist mirror reflecting nothing and by hanging a blank canvas; these were not necessarily the nihilistic acts they have sometimes been called. The determination to escape from the object, they felt, demanded such a beginning, but they fully expected to emerge on the other side with something altogether new. This was part of the Suprematist program from its inception. In May of 1915 in connection with a proposed journal, Malevich reported to Matiushin, "we intend to reduce everything to zero" but "we ourselves will then cross beyond zero."[27]

It was the need not to remain at the null point, at the total lack of form, the necessity of taking the step over the threshold from nothing into *something* again, which forced Malevich to consider the basic data available to him as a human being enmeshed forever in the cosmos. Like others of the time, Malevich regarded the human psyche as a lawful and accessible part of the natural universe, and the sensations which connected man with the rest of the world the stuff of which art should be made.

It is worthwhile making quite explicit just what Malevich understood by "sensation," *"oshchushchenie."* At times this has been translated into English as "feeling," and it has given added emotional coloring to Malevich's statements. By sensation Malevich meant an ultimately material phenomenon, but one which is subliminal. That is, an inner, physiological sensation which is so slight, so subtle, that it does not reach the threshold of physical consciousness. He saw the artist's task as cultivating these direct experiences and making them available to the intuition in its role as true creator. Their representation upon the canvas is partly a product of the ability to perceive sensation and partly a product of the state of development of the intuition, the intuitive reasoning.

Malevich began by taking as the most basic sensations color and motion and rejecting, naturally, form. And yet a painting must have form of some sort. He sought this in the medium. In *From Cubism to Suprematism* he said,

> It seems to me that it is necessary to convey purely colored motion in such a way that the picture cannot lose a single one of its colors. Motion, the running of a horse, a locomotive, can be conveyed by a monotoned pencil drawing, but not the motion of red, green and blue masses.
>
> Therefore one must turn directly to the painted masses as such, and look in them for the forms inherent to them.

Or, somewhat more dramatically,

> The human form is not intrinsic in a block of marble. Michelangelo in sculpting David did violence to the marble, he mutilated a piece of good stone. It didn't become marble, it became David.
>
> And he erred deeply if he said that he drew David out of the marble.
>
> The ruined marble was defiled first by the thought of Michelangelo about David whom he squeezed into the stone and then set free, like a splinter from a foreign body.[28]

Thus the problem of the creation of new form became the central problem of Suprematism. How does one get through to the other side of nothing? From zero to one? Malevich's solution is based on process; the artist must create *as* the universe creates:

> Nature is a living picture and we may admire her. We are the living heart of nature.
>
> We are the most valuable construction in this gigantic, living picture.
>
> We are the living brain which magnifies her life.
>
> To imitate her is theft, and her imitator is a thief; a nonentity who cannot give, but loves to take things and pass them off as his own. Counterfeits.
>
> An artist is under the obligation to be a free creator, but not a freeloader.
>
> An artist is given talent in order that he may give to life his share of creation and increase the flow of life. Only in absolute creation will he acquire his right.
>
> And this is possible when we free all our art from vulgar subject matter and teach our consciousness to see everything in nature not as real forms and objects, but as material masses from which forms must be made. . . .[29]

The forms of Suprematism were considered to have emerged from nothing in the sense of not being given forms, but rather the product of the new perception, an altered consciousness. But as such they were not arbitrary forms because they were part of the lawful processes of the psyche. As the psyche developed, by evolution and by cultivation, it had begun to distort the old perception, and forms on the canvas appeared distorted.

> Distortion was driven by the strongest people to the moment of vanishing, but it did not overstep the bounds of nothing.
>
> But I have transformed myself into the zero of form and emerged from nothing to creation, that is, to Suprematism, to the new realism in painting, to objectless creation.[30]

It is understandable that Malevich's black *Square,* the "face of the new art," his "Living Royal Infant," was in fact a square. There is no doubt that from the point of view of formal evolution Malevich had come to the square "unconsciously" as a result of his *zaum* designs for the opera *Victory Over the Sun.* There, too, the intention had been to force the viewer to abandon analytical logic in favor of direct experience, and he had experimented with sketching simple enigmatic forms in a square within a square format. Now Malevich was forced by the nature of his art to present a minimal new form, to move off the null, and the square was the least he could do: a repetition of the white edge of the canvas in black, the two planes coinciding, not even any color; from zero to one unit. One feels the rigor and the bleakness of this decision in a 1916 letter to Alexander Benois when he describes the square as the "single bare and frameless icon of our time."

Malevich produced his square as a visible unit of sensation in the new objectless consciousness. On the canvas it was not intended to be an "image" of anything, but a "living form," which like all of life multiplied by division, moving from simplicity to complexity, spawning larger and smaller Suprematist elements, neither near nor far, both static and moving, as the world was created anew, without specific objects, but certainly with all the structure and design of the natural world, including those that are inherent in man.

The step from *zaum,* which demanded of the viewer a supra-conscious act of intuition in order to perceive the cosmic relationships between objects, to Suprematism, in which the artist himself makes this intuitive triangulation, was probably not taken by Malevich until early in 1915, after Marinetti's visit and the publication in Russia of the two collections of Italian manifestos.[31] It is possible that Malevich's concept of his paintings as "living forms," i.e. reality itself rather than *images* of reality, the solution to the dilemma posed by Bergson's premise that visualization prevents perceiving the true nature of reality, was inspired by Boccioni. Portions of *Futurist Painting and Sculpture* and the *Technical Manifesto of Futurist Sculpture* may have suggested the formal vocabulary of Suprematism. Both Boccioni and Malevich were searching for an art which would spark a vision of metaphysical truths. *Zaum* had tried to do this through the juxtaposition of unrelated objects and incongruous stylistic conventions. Boccioni's proposal of a creative "plastic state of mind," through which one would create a unique form expressive of the dynamic life of an object in the universe, could not have helped but strike a responsive chord in Malevich. And Boccioni's suggestions about the nature of the form—its severity and "fundamental bareness," its inner motion rendered by straight lines of force, its extension in space, its creation of space—all seem calculated to lead Malevich ineluctably to his planar Suprematist elements. Boccioni explicitly puts forth the plane as the basis of the new form:

> In the intersecting planes of a book with the corners of a table, in the straight lines of a match, in the frame of a window, there is more truth than in all the knots of muscles, all the breasts and buttocks of heroes or Venuses. . . .[32]

Malevich seemingly had abandoned any link with the earth in favor of an act of pure creation. Intuitive forms should emerge from nothing, he had said, and "in the art of Suprematism forms will live, like all living forms of nature. . . . Each form is free and individual. Each form is a world."[33] Yet Malevich's Suprematist elements were probably not as autonomous as he claimed. Like Boccioni's sculpture they sometimes originated from transverse slices and combinations of objects, from light which cast long "suprematist" shadows, making visible cosmic and inner forces. Some of Malevich's titles for his first Suprematist pictures made reference to a subject, and perhaps also referred to Boccioni's "dynamic form," such titles as *Pictorial Realism of a Football Player, Color Masses in the Fourth Dimension,* or *Pictorial Realism of a Boy with Knapsack, Color Masses in the Fourth Dimension.*[34] In his polemic with the French Cubists about the true meaning and expression of the fourth dimension in painting, Boccioni had taken issue with their mechanistic interpretation and found the fourth dimension impossible to portray in the static and shallow Cubist space:

> Dynamic form is a species of fourth dimension, both in painting and sculpture, which cannot exist perfectly without the complete concurrence of those three dimensions which determine volume: height, width, depth.[35]

Or again:

> Through the unique form which gives continuity in space we create a form which is the sum of the potential developments of the three known dimensions. Therefore, we are not able to give a fourth dimension which is *measured and finite,* but a continuous projection of forces and forms as perceived in their infinite unfolding.[36]

Suprematism fully meets Boccioni's requirements for "Futurist space." Indeed, Boccioni's conception of a Futurist picture as a single form which produces continuity in space and which "creates sensation and involves the spectator . . . a *minimal vastness* in which depth has been substituted for the old idea of area,"[37] may exactly describe the Suprematist paintings of single planar elements.

Like Boccioni's, Malevich's understanding of the fourth dimension was associated with dynamism and with a continuity of forces and forms. But Malevich also still had in mind the old Cubo-Futurist goal of "seeing through the world," of penetration into the unified cosmos beyond the world of appearances. And just as Malevich had previously attempted to pierce the object by adopting positions unusually close to or distant from it, in 1915 he saw motion as a key into the "fourth dimensional" vision. If objects move past us rapidly enough or if we ourselves rush by them, they may seem to lose their separate identities and individual characteristics and to become a more integral part of their environment. Further, in rapid motion objects are less apt to block the view, so that it may be possible to see more easily past one row of objects to those beyond.

Beginning in the spring of 1915, Malevich maintained a regular correspondence with Matiushin, exchanging ideas about the nature of the universe and the development of a new style in art. Some parts of Malevich's side of the correspondence are now accessible, but Matiushin's contributions to the discussion are not. Some understanding about the crucial notion of the fourth dimension, however, may be gained from the following excerpt taken from one of Matiushin's notebooks and dated 29 May 1915:

> On the Fourth Dimension.
> Only motion crystallizes outward appearance into a single whole. Objectness is changed by motion. A speeding train fuses the separateness of its cars into a compact mass.
> Only the person creating connects himself, by the motion of his creation, with humanity and with the whole animal sphere in the highest ideal sense.
> Only in motion does vastness reside. The faster you move near a thick garden lattice the more clearly you see the general masses behind it. You can see in different ways simultaneously. In an elevator in motion you can see the elevator's grill, the individual objects on the wall beyond the grill, and also everything generally beyond the grill. If you ride a bicycle rapidly near a board fence, you can see the whole inner courtyard through the cracks. When at last we shall rush rapidly past objectness we shall probably see the totality of the whole world.[38]

It seems obvious from the sense and vocabulary of this statement, and from others in the same notebook, that for Malevich to depict objects without accidental features and in implied motion was, in effect, to create the fourth dimension. The objects become de-particularized, more essential, and embedded in the natural cosmic order. Henderson has convincingly argued that Malevich's actual formal vocabulary was derived from contemporary illustrations demonstrating hyperspace philosophy, particularly those found in the writings of Claude Bragdon and elaborated upon in Russia by P.D. Uspensky.[39] It also seems clear, however, that this imagery was not advocated by Matiushin in his discussions with Malevich during 1915. In his review of Malevich's work at "0-10," Matiushin was quite unaware of Bragdon and Uspensky as a source for Malevich's style, and criticized Malevich for insufficient understanding of the new dimension:

> Color should be higher than form, to the extent that it is not poured into squares, triangles, etc.[40]

In any case, Malevich felt that his resolution of the problem, his "living form," was so radical as no longer to be Futurism at all, and he renounced it at the first exhibition of his new work, "0-10," over the protests of some of his fellow exhibitors. The title given his first statement about the new style *From Cubism to Suprematism,* did not include the word Futurism, and was an attempt at compromise with his colleagues, but the full title of the exhibition itself, upon which all the exhibitors agreed, was "0-10. The Last Futurist Exhibition."

"0-10. The Last Futurist Exhibition": December 1915

"0-10. The Last Futurist Exhibition" opened at the Dobychina Gallery a few blocks from the Hermitage on the 19th of December, 1915. Through the windows, between squares painted on canvas and wooden geometrical shapes, visitors looked out upon Petrograd's ornate palaces and the stately trees of the Summer Garden, and the exhibition seemed all the more stark and bizarre. The public was incredulous; the journalists felt bored and foolish to the point of being unable to bring themselves to report what they saw. Some returned to their editors with clever copy but few with descriptions of the works.[1]

And, in fact, who could seriously describe a sculpture consisting of a white plaster ball resting in the upper right corner of an old wooden box which had been painted partly green and partly black (Puni); or elaborate on a white board, one edge cut into a semi-circle, flopped down on a windowsill (Vasileva); or a "bust" composed of a cube of cotton batting and a "hat" (Boguslavskaia)? But if this was sculpture which had become more like painting, painting had reverted to nothing but squares on canvas. Clearly, most writers understood, something had happened to the new art. This was the "Last Futurist Exhibition," they said, because the Futurists could go no further with their experiments—there was nowhere to go. This was the end of "modern" art; a return to more sensible painting—landscapes and portraits—might now be expected.

They were right in a way, not about the landscapes and portraits, but without a doubt this was the end of viable Russian Cubism and Futurism. Although among the more than one hundred and fifty works by the exhibition's fourteen artists there is little visual homogeneity, the Suprematist works revealed by Malevich and the reliefs and counter-reliefs shown by Tatlin are enough to make the exhibition a landmark of early modern art. It was the beginning of a phase so new and so fertile that its possibilities and ramifications are still being explored throughout the Western world.

"Zero-Ten" was organized by Ivan Puni, a twenty-three year old painter of independent means whose pre-1914 stylistic inclinations derived more from Western Europe than from Moscow or Petersburg. Like others of the Russian avant-garde at the beginning of World War I, Puni and his wife, Kseniia Boguslavaskaia, suddenly found themselves unable to travel between East and West and turned their attention fully to artistic activities at home. They supported financially several avant-garde projects, among them "The 'V' Trolley" exhibi-

tion in March of 1915, and "0-10" in December. At "The 'V' Trolley" Vladimir
Tatlin had shown his "painting-reliefs" from 1914 and 1915, while Malevich
exhibited works done from 1911 through 1914, the latest of which seem to be
such "Alogist" works as *Englishman in Moscow* and *Woman at a Poster
Column.*[2]

Although there is some indication that Malevich was actively in search of
a new style by late in 1914,[3] the emergence of Suprematism seems to have been
complete only in the early spring of 1915. By May, Malevich was contemplating
a journal to propagandize the new style, which already at this time was closely
associated in his mind with his 1913 sketches for *Victory Over the Sun.* In letters
which began concerning a new edition of *Victory,* Malevich wrote to Matiushin:

> Kruchenykh has told me that you are publishing "Victory Over the Sun" and that
> you want to include my drawings of the decor. I would be very grateful if you would
> include a drawing of mine for the curtain in the act where the victory took place. I
> found a draft at home and I think that now it very much needs a place in the book.
> Mention that I did the staging. Let's be printed together again. That drawing will
> have great significance in painting. That which was done unconsciously, now bears
> extraordinary fruit.[4]

> The curtain depicts a black square, the embryo of all possibilities—in its development
> it acquires a terrible strength. It is the ancestor of the cube and the sphere; its disin-
> tegration brings an amazing standard in painting. In the opera it stood for the prin-
> ciple of victory. All the many things that I staged in 1913 in your opera "Victory
> Over the Sun" gave me a mass of innovations, except no one noticed. I am collecting
> material concerning this, which ought to be published somewhere. But I need some-
> one whom I could talk to openly and who would help me set out a theory on the
> basis of its origins in painting. I think that this someone could only be you.[5]

> We are undertaking to publish a journal and beginning to discuss how and what. In
> view of the fact that in it we intend to reduce everything to zero, we have decided to
> call it *Zero.* We ourselves will then go beyond zero.

> It would be very good if you also could give us any useful advice. We will publish
> it going shares, i.e. 10 kopecks for each one, and we will publish at first two printed
> sheets—it's not much, but it's fine. . . .[6]

Malevich was so deeply involved with his new work during the summer
of 1915 that he hardly needed Puni's urging in July: "We have to paint a lot
now. The hall is very large and if we—10 people—paint 25 pictures each, then it
will only just be enough . . ."[7] Malevich worked with Ivan Kliun, Mikhail Men-
kov, Aleksei Morgunov and others, but he made an attempt to keep his work
secret from outsiders. It was, ultimately, largely unsuccessful. Toward the
end of September Puni walked into Malevich's studio unexpectedly:

I was caught like a chicken in soup. I was sitting there; I had hung up my work and was working. Suddenly the doors opened and Puni comes in. So, the work has been seen. Now no matter what, it is necessary to put out a brochure about my work and to christen it, and that way give notice of my rights as author.[8]

The consolidation of his position as the founder of a totally new direction in art depended, in Malevich's view, upon an effective explanation of the new style's philosophical underpinnings and upon the collaborative action of a group. In September and October he worked to convince his friends to publicly reject the name "Futurism" and adopt "Suprematism" at "0-10." On the day before Puni's unexpected entrance into his studio, Malevich had written to Matiushin about the reactions of his colleagues: "In Moscow they are beginning to agree with me that we have to appear under a new banner. But I just wonder, will they produce a new form?" And a few days later: "In Moscow now the critical question of creating a movement has been raised, but how and what, no one knows, and they are asking me to read something from my notes . . . . In Moscow already many people know about my works, but they just don't know anything about Suprematism. . . ."[9] As the time of the exhibition grew closer and it was necessary to make a decision, it became clear that only Malevich was ready to commit himself to the uncompromising style. "Everything has begun to turn around. The whole group of our exhibiting circle has filed a protest against the fact that I am leaving Futurism and that I want to write a few words in the catalogue and call my things Suprematism. This is the reason: 'That we all also are no longer Futurists, but we still don't know how to define ourselves, and we have too little time to think about it. . . .' "[10] Because Malevich received less than the whole hearted support of his friends, the statement to accompany his works grew to primary importance: "The brochure plays a large role for me. They have deprived me of my rights, but I'll get out of it. The name everyone knows already, but no one knows the content. *Let it be a secret.*"[11]

In the fall of 1915 Malevich believed that the new form for painting had essentially been found, and he encouraged others to search for inherent form in poetry, music and sculpture. In October, he was invited to teach, and elected to the Board, at Moscow's "Studio-Theater," a new organization which included members of the Jack of Diamonds, who, in Malevich's opinion, constituted an impossibly conservative group. At an early meeting of the Board to decide on problems of the Studio's philosophy, Malevich proceeded to lecture about Suprematist theory in music, and when this elicited disagreement, he left the organization:

It was as if I were advising crows in a field not to eat the cherries, but the grain. My stated views on music and decorative and theatrical art were received with bewilderment and as impossible because my form does not express anything. I made a big mistake when I indicated to Roslavets that contemporary music must move toward expression of the musical plastic layers and must have the length and thickness of a musical mass moving in time, while the dynamism of musical masses must give way to the static [*statizm*], i.e. to the delay in time of the musical sound mass. When they asked me where I had graduated in music, I simply quit the Board, and today I refused to teach. . . .[12]

The composer Roslavets' lack of understanding was particularly vexing to Malevich, since they had known each other as young boys and had shared an early interest in art and music:

I get so furious that he [Roslavets] writes such stuff, it seems soon I myself will give concerts just to show that this is all wrong. I keep seeing these musical masses, blocks, layers of some 20 chords hurled into space and the frozen mass of the musical cube. I genuinely hear how these 20 *pud* [271 pound] layers of sound float. . . .[13]

Malevich was equally persistent in urging his colleagues to produce Suprematist sculpture. At "0-10," Olga Rozanova showed at least two radically new sculptural works, *Automobile* and *Bicyclist (The Devil's Walk)*, but they were more "conceptual" than Suprematist in nature, and Puni's *White Ball in a Green Box*, although a very successful work, remained Cubo-Futurist. In addition to his well-known *Cubist at Her Toilet*, Ivan Kliun, according to the catalogue, exhibited at "0-10" fourteen other pieces of sculpture, only one of which, *Flying Sculpture*, bears a specific title. Seven are given the general notation, "Basic principles of sculpture," and two others, "Sculpture on a plane." Although it appears that all of these works have been lost, and no satisfactory photographs or descriptions of them have been located, it very well may be that Kliun's work at "0-10" was the first strictly Suprematist sculpture.[14]

In a curious way, even as the illusory objects were lost in Suprematism, art itself, both painting and sculpture, became the objects for eye and soul, new and universal objects that made no local compromises. That Malevich was conscious of the full implications of his work is evident from his concern not only with avoiding forms taken from visible nature but also with creation itself. It was only conventional objects that the Suprematists rejected; their own objects, made through the interaction of the introspective artist with the material world, were legitimate, lawful. The Suprematists refused to "copy nature" but they did seek essential "thingness." In his report of the lecture given by Malevich in conjunction with "0-10" Matiushin says:

Objectness carries in itself properties unknown to human intelligence, the basic essence of which may be felt not in its concrete form but rather by the intelligence altered by higher intuition. The new idea of Malevich is deeply opposed to the drawing onto the canvas vital forms held in a running start and condemned in torture to die statically in motion. Unconscious torture and pillage "from nature." The artist must now in the depths of his "I," torn from all dimensions and conventions, "conceive" from nature, in great secrecy bring forth and give birth to the still mysterious and uncopiable one who comes into the world in the harsh torment of joyful service to a new embodiment on earth.[15]

Malevich's painting, and presumably also Suprematist sculpture and music, were understood by Matiushin and others as a "higher order" of expression which, while existing as earthly works of art, at the same time took a "more valid" stance in their orientation to the universe. An "absolute" art of a revelatory nature was a goal of several of the occult sciences of the period, and connections between them and Russian and other modern styles, both in painting and literature, have been well established.[16] Occult sciences gave the artist a new complete mythology which incorporated the latest scientific discoveries into ancient and Eastern wisdom, and in doing so suggested a universal and essential art. Such systems of mystified science without exception placed great emphasis on the artist and his role in bringing spiritual enlightenment to his audience. In practise, works of art became "experiments" or "examples" which demonstrated the new world view as well as depicted it, and as a result, much of the new art functions successfully as both object and sign.

Since the mid-1920's art historians have been pleased to disassociate the development of abstraction from mystical and spiritual influences which from that time were considered anti-formalist or anti-rational, and therefore unworthy of serious scholarly consideration. Studies initiated in the past ten years, however, have begun to establish a more balanced view.[17] The "spiritual," as it was understood by Malevich and Kandinsky and countless other artists of the time, was not merely "spiritualistic," but rather that quality which expresses the highest human potential and which includes all the forms of knowledge to which man aspires and which raise him above other forms of life. Perhaps the best translation that English can offer is "the human spirit." Misunderstanding of the multifaceted nature of the modern artists' spiritual orientation is a result, in part, of the contemporary Western dichotomy of vision. It is useless to insist, as some historians continue to do, that modernists were members of either the rational or anti-rational camp. At the turn of the century no such well delineated camps existed. For a quarter of a century both poets and scientists strove for a holistic vision; the mystical world view and that of the new physical and biological sciences emphasized the unity of knowledge and presented the artist with strikingly similar and visual suggestions.

Such a unified conception of the world, whether derived from physics, mathematics and physiology, or Theosophy, Anthroposophism and the teachings of P.D. Uspensky, reinforced the breakdown of barriers between artistic media. Modernism turned upon "synthetic" approaches to art modelled after the new knowledge. Malevich, in his struggle with *zaum,* had prepared himself to see the philosophical, and to a lesser extent the visual consequences of the new style.

For him it was not only a breakthrough into the objectless world of painting, but the complete, synthetic system that had been the goal of the avant-garde, especially the Russian Cubo-Futurists, for some time. It is indicative of these holistic aspirations that Malevich thought immediately of Suprematist sculpture, poetry and music, and that in future years he would return repeatedly to *Victory Over the Sun* as a work which offered the simultaneous expression of all three forms of art.

Malevich's other deep and immediate concern was to place Suprematism within the context of the history of art. His motivation was not only the desire to validate Suprematism historically, and himself as founder. His earlier stylistic innovations had not moved him in this way. But in 1915 Malevich felt immediately the immensity of his decision and part of his commitment to it was based on what he felt to be its historical inevitability. In his desire to make clear the organic evolutionary principles which dictated objectless painting, he gradually developed a formal method of stylistic analysis that was pioneering in its approach to style and to pedagogical method. His later inability, or more likely lack of desire, to develop fully the visual implications of Suprematism was at least partly due to the aim of his method of analysis. From the beginning Malevich's historical context was based on the assumption that external form in art gives evidence of psychic or psychological states of being and of physiological evolution. Underlying Malevich's history of style is a fundamental psychological, rather than visual, absolutism.

As we have seen, Malevich and the other artists of the avant-garde were quite aware of Western European developments in art. The principal Russian contributors to their esthetic theories were Kulbin, Kruchenykh, Markov and Matiushin. Some further examination of particular aspects of the ideas of these men should help to clarify and summarize the evolution of Suprematism.

All of Kulbin's theories are concerned with the psychological impact of the work of art, and have as a fundamental premise a pan-psychic view of the world. Everything is alive, Kulbin believed, even the rocks and other inorganic objects. The life which exists in all things is at bottom based on the interrelationship of harmonies and dissonances. Harmony is correctness of relationships, symmetry; but an object such as a crystal, which is completely harmonious, appears to be "dead." The more obvious manifestations of life are associated with complication of form, and hence with "dissonance." In the plastic arts, as in other arts, dissonance excites the perceiver, while consonance calms him. For Kulbin, the affective value of a work of art was a result of sensations which are physically based but 'unconscious.' Such sensations act directly on the brain of the perceiver without his conscious knowledge and so the effect is singularly powerful.[18]

For maximum affectiveness Kulbin advocated the use of "close combinations" of colors, that is, combinations of colors which are near to one another in the spectrum. Because of the physical interaction of such colors, which may be seen in interference phenomena, for example, they are "dissonant" and so act strongly on the feelings of the viewer. The fact that the viewer is hardly conscious of the physical interaction of "close combinations" of colors, or even that there is in fact any difference between them, only makes them all the more powerful. He maintained that these subtle dissonances and close combinations were one of the distinguishing characteristics of the new art. Another of the new art's special properties, and a prime cause of its extreme affectiveness, was, according to Kulbin, its great economy of means. The senses leave particular traces in the brain, he said, and the new styles are a projection outward of what has been laid down inside. The painting actually resembles the "sign" present in the brain of the artist, and as such makes immediate appeal to the viewer.[19]

It should be noted that Kulbin's is a curious combination of scientific Impressionist and German psychological theories of color. He is interested both in the physical action of color and its psychological effect on the viewer, but he does not pursue very far the idea of purely subjective associations. Just once or twice does he make a gesture toward associational characterization of color, but it is so distant from his physically based approach to analysis that he soon abandons it. Although he does not say so specifically, his discussion of such phenomena as interference shows that he thought of color primarily in terms of light, and so he is concerned with additive mixing. But for Kulbin the mixing did not occur in the *eye,* but rather in the "higher psychological centers."[20] In place of an emphasis on the mechanisms of optical mixing he substitutes 'psychological mixing.' Thus, he says that actually the dissonances received by the viewer are ultimately resolved in an accord; they are matched, he says, to the natural dissonance, that vital complexity present in man's soul.

The sources of Kulbin's esthetic theories are fairly clear. He is primarily concerned with "psychophysics" and his definition of it as the "physics of the soul"[21] betrays a familiarity with contemporary German psychology, particularly with Wilhelm Wundt and his associates who also identified the soul with psychic activity.[22] The term psycho-physics originated with Wundt's friend and precursor Gustav Fechner who, in his *Elements of Psychophysics,*[23] applied the tools of physics to an investigation of the subjective effects of sensory stimulation. By the end of the century Fechner's great two volume work had been republished and had become a standard text for students in the sciences.[24]

Kulbin's references to color sensations that are not even conscious assume Fechner's "subliminal consciousness" which he believed to exist below the threshold of feeling. Fechner had experimented with many kinds of threshold phenomena, including faint shades of color. Kulbin might also have known Leibniz's similar argument for infinitely small sensations of which the subject is unaware.[25]

Kulbin's pan-psychism seems to have been inspired by another of Fechner's ideas: that we live in an animate universe in which life exists in all things "in potential"; like Kulbin, Fechner described the inorganic world as merely "sleeping." Matter, he said, is only the outward manifestation of a universal consciousness, of which our own subliminal consciousness partakes. Although Kulbin never described his conception of the universe very thoroughly, his ideas appear to coincide with Fechner's in several respects; in general both considered psychic life a transcendental principle which was closely associated with the structure of matter.

Another source for Kulbin's "small intervals" or "close combinations" of colors with special affective powers may have been a book which he apparently knew but never mentions: Ogden Rood's *Modern Chromatics.*[26] In his discussion of contrast and gradation in this work, Rood introduces the notion that colors can be made richer and more effective by juxtaposing those that are "distant from each other in the chromatic circle by a *small interval.*"[27] Much of Kulbin's exposition of the advantages of this method of color selection, as well as certain other references, points to a knowledge of this book. In the chapter on the small interval, Rood advises the artist to train himself to "acquire the power of consciously tracing fainter gradations of color" and notes that the unconscious is already aware of these small intervals.

> We are in the habit of thinking of a sheet of paper as being quite uniform in tint, and yet instantly reject as insufficient such a representation of it. In this matter our unconscious education is enormously in advance of our conscious. . . . It is one of the tasks of the artist to ascertain the causes that give rise to the highly complex sensations which he experiences . . .[28]

Rood's approach to color and to art in general must have been very congenial to Kulbin since it was that of a physicist who studied painting and himself painted as a serious hobby. Rood, an American, had studied both physics and painting in Germany[29] and his work on color was well known to Seurat and other Neo-Impressionists.[30] In addition to English, *Modern Chromatics* appeared in German and French.[31]

For his discussion of the dissonances produced by the interaction of wave phenomena among such "close combinations," Kulbin is strongly indebted to Hermann Helmholtz's work in acoustics and music. Kulbin himself did his first and most detailed esthetics in the development of his theory of "free music," wherein the notion of dissonances and small intervals was also advanced. In *On the Sensations of Tone*[32] Helmholtz had given a detailed exposition of dissonant intervals and beats, and furthermore had pointed out that dissonances are an important means of expression and contrast.

That which is physically agreeable is an important adjunct and support to esthetic beauty, but it is certainly not identical with it. On the contrary, in all arts we frequently employ its opposite, that which is physically disagreeable, partly to bring the beauty of the first into relief, by contrast, and partly to gain a more powerful means for the expression of passion. Dissonances are used for similar purposes in music. They are partly means of contrast, to give prominence to the impression made by consonances, and partly means of expression, not merely for peculiar and isolated emotional disturbances, but generally to heighten the impression of musical progress and impetuosity, because when the ear has been distressed by dissonances it longs to return to the calm current of pure consonances.[33]

It seems possible that Kulbin combined Helmholtz's work on intervals and the expressiveness of dissonance in music with a variation of Rood's notion of small color intervals or Fechner's "just observable" differences. The basis for the affectiveness of these phenomena Kulbin sought in current physiological theory. Even the seemingly strange idea of the picture as a "symbol" projected from within the artist's brain is derived from Wundt and Helmholtz.[34]

By understanding psyche as an accessible part of the natural universe, Kulbin bridged the gap between the affective and objective world with the work of art. His conception of color as both sense and sensation made it an essential link in his sweeping theory of form and feeling. He was especially significant as a highly visible and vocal source in Russia for the esthetic reverberations of German psychology and physiology.

Matiushin's approach to esthetics had much in common with Kulbin's. Although he does not appear to have believed in a specifically animate universe, the main impetus in all of his work is a quest for the same sort of underlying principle with which to encompass knowledge advanced by both art and science, and so to render the universe whole. Instead of psychology and physiology, Matiushin looked to geometry and mathematics for his unifying principle; but along with Kulbin he too believed that the new styles were somehow more faithful in their reflection of something physically real, and he tried to offer a rational explanation for art without being "restrictive' in the application of rules. The artist's main task, according to Matiushin, was the penetration of a higher reality through the development of a heightened awareness, and this took not intuition, but conscious study, training, and work.

Matiushin's ideas about the new art either originated from or coincided with many of those expressed by Gleizes and Metzinger in *Du Cubisme*. Matiushin was their first Russian translator,[35] and he seems to have taken their interpretation of Cubism so to heart that for twenty years after its publication his work may be understood as an attempt to establish a scientific and objective basis for their statements. In common with the other Russian artists and writers at the turn of the century, Matiushin understood the artist as 'seer.'

> Artists have always been knights, poets and prophets of space, in all times; sacri-
> ficing to everyone, dying, they were opening eyes and teaching the crowd to see the
> great beauty of the world concealed from it. So also now; Cubism has raised the flag
> of the New World, of the new learning about the merging of time and space.[36]

Matiushin took the idea of vision literally, and eventually in a long essay, "An
Artist's Experience of the New Space" (1926), he tried to teach the artist to
see with each eye independently in order to broaden the angle of vision, to
purposefully develop a kind of strabismus, in order to understand how relative
is our ordinary vision. For Matiushin this "widened viewing" was a way of
plunging into that "profound reality" of which *Du Cubisme* spoke. In order to
see colors more luminously, Matiushin advised looking with a wide but glancing
view, without fixing them with the eye or any accommodation of the vision.

Matiushin's interest in color, he says in his memoirs, began before 1905
when he was painting in a Neo-Impressionist style, and experimenting with
effects of light and shadow. Later we find him demanding that color should be
more dynamic and "self-sufficient," and admonishing Malevich for putting too
little emphasis on color in his Suprematist pictures.[37] Behind Matiushin's insistence on color was the belief that color vision was evolving in man, and that
gradually the color-receiving cones in the eye would spread from the center
of the retina toward its periphery. Thus man is developing a capacity for better
color vision, especially for seeing colored objects in motion (the perception of
motion being especially acute on the periphery of the retina). An artist whose
vision had been trained in this direction could gain an inkling of the new consciousness and a truer understanding of the nature of reality.

"Every inflection of form is accompanied by a modification of color, and
every modification of color gives birth to a form," *Du Cubisme* had stated, and
Matiushin's most substantial work on color seems to have been an attempt to
verify this objectively and to determine the natural laws which govern the inter-
dependence of form and color. In his book, *The Natural Law of Changeability
in Color Combinations*,[38] Matiushin reported on his experiments with models of
simple forms and colors in a controlled environment. By altering one or more
conditions of the environment or the method of viewing, he observed deforma-
tions in both color and form of the models. Again it was the interconnectedness
of things that fascinated Matiushin, the universal connections which were mani-
fested as deformation in objects, more specifically in forms and colors: if the
artist could perceive these he could hope to give concrete visual form to his more
advanced understanding.

Vladimir Markov's "Principles of the New Art"[39] anticipated Malevich's
interpretation of the creative process so closely that it seems highly unlikely
that Malevich did not know it. As Malevich would later do, Markov emphasized
the "instinctive wisdom" of the artist as he creates freely and playfully, without
"utilitarian" purpose. He judged contemporary Europe to be very poor in de-

veloping viable plastic principles, and saw it instead as endlessly reworking the old ones which "by their very nature, confine creativity within a narrow bewitched circle." Again anticipating Malevich, Markov cautioned against understanding "sincerity" in a superficial sense; fools and fashion followers have no artistic value, even though they may be sincere. Sincerity must be founded on "internal necessity," on the "order of the soul." He distinguishes three stages of the artist's "I": the concealed, unconscious, but nevertheless individual "I"; the concealed but conscious, and hence more mature, "I"; and, most importantly in art, the outward manifestation of the first two. It must not be expected that art will be a perfect expression of the conscious and unconscious personality of the artist, but, Markov suggests, inhibiting factors may be identified by "criticism and other means." He then lists several factors which affect the outward expression of the artist's psyche, notions that Malevich would make use of after the Revolution in his theory of education. Thus, according to Markov, the artist should not strive to imitate nature, express his "self," or liberate his energy. The forms of art are rather a synthesis of complex analyses and sensations; they embody the artist's design relative to nature and the inner world of his "I." In Markov's "free creation" an artist depicts an object not as he sees it, but as he feels it. Behind the surface of an object is its rhythm which an artist feels and which his forms make manifest. Outward expression is valued for "its analogous rhythm, its beauty, equipollent to the forgotten object." Seemingly coarse or absurd objects may have "inner beauty, rhythm and harmony." But the artist is not restricted to any consideration of the object. He "has a right to play with all worlds accessible to him: both the world of objects, and the world of forms, lines, colors, and light." From the point of view of naturalism the forms may

> . . . appear as quite free and arbitrary, but this does not exclude the fact that they can be strictly constructive from the point of view of aesthetic requirements.
>
> Free creation is the mother of art. Free creation raises us above "this world". . . . The aspiration to other worlds is inherent in man's nature. Man . . . strains toward the sky. The surest path to the sky is free creation.[40]

In this work Markov not only recognized the emotional content of rhythms and relationships, those derived from objects as well as those which are purely abstract, but he very specifically mentions art as a product of intuition and thus a reflection of a "divine" principle. Since intuition contains some aspect of fundamental truth, modern artists may give expression to their unconscious, wild, primitive instincts. Yet, he notes, esthetically the product may be "strictly constructive." It was probably to Markov's and Kulbin's ideas about intuition and coarseness that Kruchenykh refers in his *Declaration of the Word as Such* (written in April 1913, and published in the summer).

Although he mentions the inner rhythm of objects, Markov showed no reticence about abandoning the object immediately and completely. He did not advocate (as did Kandinsky at this time) "concealing" the objects or even reducing them to signs or symbols. Markov's approach to art is permeated by a sense of freedom and joy which finds expression in metaphors of flying:

> And only narrow-minded doctrinaires and dunder-headed Philistines can demand that art . . . should not burst the dam of realism and depart for the endless horizons of free creation.[41]

Malevich, with Kruchenykh, followed Markov's path to absurdity and alogism, and also arrived finally at the same "endless horizons of free creation." We hear a decisive and affirmative echo of Markov in the introduction to Malevich's objectless Suprematist style:

> I have destroyed the ring of the horizon and escaped from the circle of things, from the horizon-ring which confines the artist and the forms of nature.[42]

Although Malevich later may have rejected as spurious the more explicit post-Revolutionary "aerial Suprematism," it is striking that consistently the most recurrent sensation mentioned by Malevich in connection with Suprematism is that of height and space.

> The ascent to the heights of non-objective art is arduous and painful . . . but it is nevertheless rewarding. The familiar recedes ever further and further into the background. . . . The contours of the objective world fade more and more and so it goes, step by step, until finally the world—"everything we loved and by which we have lived"—becomes lost to sight.[43]

For Malevich, art was the communication of sensation.[44] By this he meant not ordinary conscious feeling, but the inner psychological, yet physically based, sensation, the notion current in German psychology, of which Kulbin had spoken. The concept of subliminal sensation is just one of Kulbin's ideas that Malevich shared. With Kulbin, Malevich considered that the picture comes from within and is a product of biology and psyche. He regarded color as closely associated with sensation, and under certain circumstances, virtually identical with it.

> The picture—paint, color—lies inside our organism.
> My nervous system is colored by them.
> My brain burns with their color.[45]

That which is seen is selected unconsciously, analyzed consciously, and then transformed by the organism, the "intuition" or "imagination." Works of art, Malevich believed, are products of psychological changes of perception, not mere optical alterations of reality. Malevich therefore proposed that the problem be treated by "psychophysiology."[46] In spite of the fact that Matiushin was probably close philosophically to Fechner and his heirs, who assumed that by measuring subjective reactions to external stimuli one indeed included the responses of the psyche, he later limited his discussion of his work to pointing out the practical uses for the observed phenomena. Malevich, however, had no pressing need for such information, and although he did accept Matiushin's later work on color as physical fact, he cautioned that such information must be transformed, just like all other external knowledge, within the "imagination" of the artist.

But, like Kulbin and Matiushin, it was color which Malevich believed to be the primary impetus in the new art. He grew conscious of the fact that color was perceived by the imagination apart from the objects in which it inhered. Yet even so it was forced, at the beginning, to make do with the old forms:

> But color was oppressed by common sense, it was enslaved by it. And the spirit of color grew weak and died out.
> But when it conquered common sense, then the colors flowed into the form of the real things which they hated.
> The colors had matured, but their form had not matured in the consciousness.
> That is why faces and bodies were red, green, and blue.[47]

Gradually the old forms began to give way. The more intense and expressive the sensation, the more it became conscious, the more the objects were deformed within the artist. Malevich later made diagrams of this process,[48] which show three concentric circles representing the three steps in color perception: the outer circle indicates the color stimuli themselves, next their effect on the optical perception, and then to the "center of distribution." Only after these three stages of perception have been completed are the forms or objects for the colors selected. As the artist, through cultivation of his sensitivity or through evolution itself, becomes more aware of strong sensations, the objects in his work become increasingly distorted and gradually disappear.[49] At first only the signs of objects are left, as in the work of Cezanne or in the first stages of Cubism, but finally there comes a time when sensation is so powerful that all traces of the object disappear. In his 1915 publication *From Cubism to Suprematism* Malevich stated explicitly that it is the sensations of color and motion which go in search of form:

> It seems to me that it is necessary to convey purely colored motion in such a way that the picture cannot lose a single one of its colors. . . . One must turn directly to the painted masses as such, and look in them for the forms inherent to them.[50]

In Suprematism objects have gone completely; only their sensations are left, conveyed by the relationship of the elements: the dynamics, the spatial relationships and color contrasts. It is these sensations which may convey something essential about the universe.

The process of artistic evolution, then, is the process of the artist's intuition or psyche becoming more and more sensitive. As Kulbin had recommended combinations of colors close in the spectrum to appeal subliminally to the psyche of the viewer, Malevich's Suprematism detected more and more subtle contrasts of sensation in the artist. The "white on white" series of paintings in 1917-1918 reflected an exquisite refinement of sensation and appealed for ever more finely tuned reception by the viewer. Inevitably the distinctions become too slight for visual perception.[51] Going one step further than Kulbin, Malevich wanted to touch the viewer without material at all: the result should be an explosion of sensation.

If we examine Malevich's work at the time of origin of Suprematism, we find verification of his description of the role of color in the emergence of these objectless paintings. An equally important role, it seems, was played by light in his drawings. As we have seen, Malevich probably began to work with light during the production of the opera *Victory Over the Sun*. Projected light seemed to fragment and animate objects and render individual segments autonomous. He experimented also with drawn intersecting rays of light. In *Simultaneous Death in an Airplane and at the Railway,* there are intersecting shafts of light that fall across the picture to create a maze of overlapping planes, an effect similar in principle to the colored planes of Larionov's early Rayist works. One of the most striking examples of this approach to implied light was Malevich's drawing which appeared in Matiushin's publication *The Three.* It too is a depiction of light action, but in this case the shadows are revelatory and the planar unmodulated Suprematist elements begin to emerge. A comparison of this drawing with the design for a book cover done seven years later clearly shows the genesis of Suprematism.[52]

Such works show that Suprematism was not so much a search for spiritual essences or a reductivist process, as an attempt to construct, to assemble, a vision of that which exists beneath the threshold of the senses, to look at the world so intensely as to see it all. By casting it in a bright new light, Suprematism hoped to penetrate the old limits of sensitivity. As Matiushin had recommended a glancing vision in order to catch the most beautiful and elusive colors, Malevich used a sidewise glance to force objects to cast their shadow into a new reality.

In the same way as the Suprematist elements began to emerge in these drawings as volumetric modeling gave way, so in the paintings the modeling grew more and more abrupt in color changes until the stripes of color began to assume a significance of their own. The clear reds, greens, blues and yellows of Malevich's Fauvist pictures of 1911 appear again the following year in such works as *Taking in the Rye,* but now they are used for severe volumetric modeling and there is some blending, but little mixing of colors. Some of the rounded shapes, the back of the upper left hand woman, for example, present almost a complete color spectrum. The hat of the man in *Englishman in Moscow* is composed of two stripes: green and black. With such "self-sufficient" colors condensing into stripes, Malevich must indeed have felt that he had colors in search of a form. One can easily imagine those bright strips floating out from the objects where they were imprisoned—to swim in the freedom of the objectless world of Suprematism, free finally from the skirts and shirts and faces.

Color relationships and contrasts in paintings such as *Taking in the Rye* were already ends in themselves, and structural rather than emotional. It could not be long before they asserted that self-sufficiency. Unlike Kandinsky, Malevich never conceived of color as related to modes or particular emotions. For Malevich, they were expressive only of the psychological constitution which in turn was governed externally by environment and internally by physical and psychological maturity. Such things were a matter of external reality on the one hand and growth and evolution on the other, and were far from 'intuitively' based in the usual sense. In Malevich's esthetics we can detect Kulbin's concern with psychological dynamics and Matiushin's fascination with color and motion, and especially his overwhelming sense of limitless space. Suprematism was a joyful expression of Russia's greatest dream: the continuity of man with his universe:

> Then will the rhythm of the cosmic sensation be fully perceived, then the entire world will be embedded in an enclosure of eternal sensation, in the rhythm of the cosmic infinite of a dynamic silence.[53]

From the foregoing discussion it is possible to venture a few observations about the Western art currents relevant to Russian objectless art, and about the nature of Russian modernism itself. Both Kulbin and Malevich are indebted to German esthetic and psychological ideas current after about 1860. It should be noted that in both Germany and France at this time scientists and estheticians were often the same people, that scientists lectured freely on art, and that estheticians aspired to the scientific method. It is a trend which continues today. As their name indicated, the Russian Cubo-Futurists believed themselves related to the French Cubists and the Italian Futurists. But in the realm of ideas they seem to have been highly selective about what they adopted from these two movements. Although at first they undoubtedly benefited from the new formal innovations, the Russian artists were not then primarily interested in the intricacies of Cubism's plastic conventions of representing the natural world, nor in the technological side of Futurism. The authors of *Du Cubisme,* a treatise very congenial to the Russian spirit, were philosophically idealistic and had been strongly influenced by Symbolism, a style which in literature in the early years of the twentieth century had risen to the level of religious belief in Russia, and which had sunk deep into every subsequent artistic development in that country. While the Russian modernists had no desire to return into the 'mystical mists' of early Symbolism, the notion of another, 'more real' world which might be penetrated only by the artist was as important for them as it was for Gleizes and Metzinger. With Futurism they shared a communal utopianism, but this, too, had long been part of the Russian tradition.[54] Their interest in color specifically derives from Scientific Impressionism and its continuation in the psychological aspects of color theory. They seem to have been less interested in the purely intuitive or subjective approach to color, although the influence of this school of ideas may be found in an emphatic concern for the communication of the artist's feeling.[55]

Malevich and his friends have often been understood as proposing an 'absolute' or a 'mystical' art; actually they seem to have avoided such extremes. While they spoke of the artist's relationship to all of nature and, like the Symbolists, dreamt of somehow aligning themselves with the universe so that art would function as a 'bridge' between man and the rest of the world, they looked to science, not to emotionalism or mysticism, for a way to proceed. Reality no longer had to be approached through hermetic systems of correspondences. Malevich had reversed directions. Reality and the external world could now surely be found within each person, directly accessible and knowable. Bergson had given the artist reality again, but it was now neither mechanical nor naturalistic; it gave the artist a basis for order without the restraints of either absolute or representational systems. Malevich never considered Suprematism a visually absolute art; he was too conscious of its dependence upon the individual creative principle. But on the other hand, the work of art stood in a definite relation to the external world, so it might be considered for itself and without reference to the psychology of the viewer. "Forms must be given life and the right to individual existence," he said, and it was this aspect of Malevich's thinking which made possible the careful formal analyses of style which he carried out after the Revolution. In 1927 he gave a very concise description of this understanding of the work of art:

> For us painting has become the body wherein are put forth the reasons and mental condition of the painter, the structure of his understanding of nature, and the relationship between himself and the actions of nature.[56]

For Malevich, Suprematism was the leading edge of human perception, a gateway to the real, the objectless, world.

> You are in the nets of the horizon, like fish! We, Suprematists, throw open the way to you. Hurry!—For tomorrow you will not recognize us.[57]

Notes

Introduction

1. There are several similar paintings of Malevich's square in Russian museums. The Tretyakov Gallery in Moscow has *Black Suprematist Square,* 31 1/8 inches square, probably the original *Square* shown in the "0-10" exhibition. It also has a copy made in 1929 for his retrospective at the Tretyakov that year, with the same title, of almost the same size, 31 1/2 inches square. The Russian Museum in Leningrad owns a larger *Black Square,* 43 inches square, and a *Red Square/Peasant Woman–Suprematism,* 20 7/8 inches square, as well as *Black Circle,* 43 inches square, and *Cross-Shaped Suprematism,* a black cross, 43 3/8 inches square.

   Although there is no documented evidence that a circle painting appeared in "0-10," it is known that paintings of other simple geometric shapes were shown: a cross, a long horizontal rectangle and a vertically oriented trapezoidal figure. There were most likely others.

2. Malevich's Suprematist works were shown throughout Europe during the 1920's. Even during the twenties Suprematist ideas passed naturally into luminism and kineticism, and Malevich's impact on the Bauhaus School can be seen in the work of such artists as Hans Richter and Laszlo Moholy-Nagy. This tradition has surfaced more recently in the work of such artists as Yves Klein and the Zero group–Gunther Uecker, Heinz Mack and Otto Piene–which makes no secret of its indebtedness to Malevich. His legacy is also still alive in the Soviet Union, for example in the work of the Leningrad "Sterligov Group," in some of the work of the Moscow painter Viktor Pivovarev, and in the former "Dvizhenie (Movement) Group," led by Lev Nusberg (emigrated 1976). In 1967 Nusberg stated:

   > To this day I greatly admire Kazimir Malevich. No artist (with the possible exception of Klee) has had a greater influence on me, a blessed influence! He summed up all "classical" plastic art. "Statements by Kinetic Artists," *Studio International* 173 no. 886 (February, 1967): 60.

3. The Société Anonyme has shown Malevich's Suprematist works in the United States since the 1920's. The question of Suprematism and American Post-Expressionism is treated in: Max Kozloff, "Malevich as a Counter-revolutionary (East and West)," *Artforum,* XII, 5 (January, 1974): 30; Clement Greenberg, *Post-Painterly Abstraction,* (Los Angeles, 1964); Donald Judd, "Malevich: Independent Form, Color, Surface" *Art in America,* 62, 2 (March/April, 1974): 52; in addition see Lawrence Alloway, "Systemic Painting," Barbara Rose, "ABC Art," Willoughby Sharp, "Luminism and Kineticism" all reprinted in *Minimal Art: A Critical Anthology,* Gregory Battcock, ed. (NY, 1968).

4. Descriptions of several of these pieces will be found in Chapter 5. At the time of "Zero-Ten" the press reported that Puni exhibited "without any commentary, an ordinary board about 3 1/2 by 14 inches, painted green." (Berninger, Cartier, *Pougny* (Tubingen, 1972): 60-61. A flirtation with conceptual principles may be seen in Malevich's assertion that Suprematist pictures might be produced by phoning a sign painter with dimensions. Alloway (in "Systemic Painting") sees Malevich's pencil renditions of his paintings in *The Objectless World* as a conceptualist act.

5. For a careful explication of Malevich's relationship to Uspensky see Linda Dalrymple Henderson, "The Merging of Time and Space: The 'Fourth Dimension' in Russia from Ouspensky to Malevich," *Soviet Union* 5, pt. 2 (1978): 171-203. This article derives in part from a broader consideration of the role of idealized science in modern art in Henderson's unpublished dissertation, *The Artist, 'The Fourth Dimension', and Non-Euclidean Geometry 1900-1930: A Romance of Many Dimensions* (Yale University, 1975).

6. *Die gegenstandslose Welt*, Bauhausbucher no. 11, H. von Riesen, trans. (Munich, 1927); *The Non-Objective World*, H. Dearstyne, trans. (Chicago, 1959). A more complete text of this and many other writings by Malevich has recently appeared in English in the four volumes edited by Troels Andersen: K.S. Malevich, *Essays on Art: 1915-1933* I, 11 (Chester Springs, Penn., 1969), *The World as Non-Objectivity* III (Copenhagen, 1976), *The Artist, Infinity, Suprematism* IV (Copenhagen, 1978).

7. Troels Andersen, *Malevich, Catalogue Raisonné of the Berlin Exhibition 1927* (Amsterdam, 1970).

8. Donald Gordon, *Modern Art Exhibitions 1900-1916* I (Munich, 1974): 34.

Chapter 1

1. *Zolotoe Runo* 5 (1908): 74. *Khudozhniki narodov SSSR* I (M, 1970): 429. (The date of the exhibition is here given incorrectly as 1907.) In the exhibition catalogue Bogdanov-Belsky is listed among the "Neo-realists." The exhibition contained more than 400 works contributed by six groups, and included eight works by a blind artist. The opening day of the exhibition is confirmed by an invitation kept in the archives of the Russian Museum, f. 121, ed. khr. 117, no. 51.

2. *Vesna. (Spring, The organ of independent writers and artists.)* Published by N.G. Shebuev. Kamensky was editor of eleven issues published in St. Petersburg in 1908. *Bibliografii periodicheskikh izdanii Rossii, 1901-1916* I (L, 1958): 160-61.

3. Vasilii Kamenskii, *Put' entuziasta* (M, 1931): 103.

4. Ibid., 100. Breshko-Breshkovsky was known—semi-affectionately—among the avantgarde as "Breshko from Birzhovki"; Chukovsky and another journalist, Petr Pil'skii, were called "Pil'chukovskii" and "Chukopil'skii." *Zolotoe Runo* 11/12 (1909): 90; Kamenskii, *Put'*: 100.

5. "Vystavki," *Zolotoe Runo* 5 (1908): 74.

6. Kamenskii, *Put'*: 100-101.

7. S. Sudeikin, *Kul'bin* (SP, 1912): 33. This date seems to be the most reliable available; Kulbin's age is given variously by several memoirists, usually as older than his birth date would indicate.

8. *Stoletie voennago ministerstva 1802-1902* T. VIII, SP; 1, 1902; II, 1908; III, 1909; IV, 1911. Kulbin's medical publications date from 1894 and include more than a dozen titles, most having to do with observing the psycho-physical effects of irritants on

organisms. In this he was following the most advanced medical interests of the period, including those of the famous Ivan Pavlov. Kulbin's medical researches culminated with the publication in 1907 of a booklet entitled *Sensitivity. Essays in Psychometry and the Clinical Application of its Data [Chuvstvitel'nost. Ocherki po psikhometrii i klinicheskomu primeneniiu eia dannykh]* (SP: 1907). Kulbin's medical experiments are closely related to his esthetic theories.

9. Kulbin received his general's rank in 1907.

10. The Catalogue for "An Exhibition of Modern Trends" listed each painter's affiliation. Eduard Spandikov and Iosif Shkol'nik, soon to be associated with "The Union of Youth," are here in Kulbin's "△". Burliuk's "Wreath," besides the three Burliuks, included Vasilii Kuznetsov (sculpture), Lentulov and Exter. Burliuk includes a note on the first exhibition of "Wreath" held in Moscow the previous December and January. Burliuk was probably attempting to distinguish his exhibitions from the large exhibition with the same title, "Wreath," which opened in St. Petersburg exactly one month before "Modern Trends" on 24 March 1908. Although there were some contributors common to the December-January Moscow exhibition and that in St. Petersburg in March, the Burliuks did not participate in the latter. *Katalog. Vystavka "Sovremennykh techenii v iskusstve"* (SP, 1908). *Katalog kartin vystavki "Venok" 1908g.* (SP, 1908). Late in 1908 D. Burliuk and A. Exter arranged an exhibition of "Wreath" in Kiev; in addition to the three Burliuks, participants included Larionov, Goncharova, Lentulov and Fon Vizen. At this exhibition Burliuk distributed a statement entitled, "The Voice of an Impressionist in Defense of Painting." *K istorii russkago avangarda,* N. Khardzhiev, ed. (Stockholm, 1976): 73 n. 45.

11. Georgii Ivanov, *Peterburgskie zimy* (NY, 1952): 38-39. Although his memoirs are often unreliable, Ivanov's description of Kulbin here sounds very characteristic.

12. Sudeikin, *Kul'bin:* 33.

13. D. Burliuk, "Nasha pervaia zima v Petere," *Color and Rhyme:* 55, 26.

14. Kamensky at this time had already been in Petersburg a year and a half, attending the Higher Agricultural School. Born in 1884 on a steamer on the Kama River, Kamensky was orphaned before he was of school age and brought up in Perm by his mother's sister. His literary endeavors began at seventeen with newspaper articles about local social problems. Kamensky also had a brief career as an actor in 1903-1904, but gave it up, supposedly on the advice of Meyerhold who had employed him as an extra in the provincial town of Nikolaev. See V. Kamenskii, *Kak ia zhil i zhivu* (Tiflis, 1927): 5-6.

15. D. Burliuk, "Nasha pervaia zima . . . ,": 26. Lentulov had come recently to Petersburg from Penza. Since he had failed the entrance examination for the Academy of Arts, he was at this time studying with D.N. Kardovsky. His first exhibition in St. Petersburg would be with Burliuk (and Sudeikin, Sapunov, Goncharova and Larionov) in the "Wreath" exhibit of 1909. I.E. Grabar', *Istoriia russkogo iskusstva* X, kn. 2aia (M, 1969): 114; M.A. Lentulova, *Khudozhnik Aristarkh Lentulov* (M, 1969): 9ff.

16. "Staroe i molodie na poslednikh vystavkakh" in *Zolotoe Runo* 1 (1908): 89.

17. Khlebnikov's poems were accepted, and thus *Vesna* has the honor of having first published his verse, in no. 9 (Oct. 1908).

Khlebnikov entered St. Petersburg University as a fifth semester student in the physico-mathematics faculty in September 1908. He changed officially to the historical-philological faculty in October 1909. *Sobranie proizvedenii Velimir Khlebnikova* 5, N. Stepanov, ed. (L, 1933): 357-58.

18. V. Kamenskii, *Put'.* 107; *Kak ia zhil i zhivu:* 6. Kamensky also said he studied literature with Burliuk.

19. D. Burliuk, *Color and Rhyme,* 57: 1. Also Katherine S. Drier, *Burliuk* (N.Y., 1944): 52. Burliuk's reports of the size of Kulbin's show are greatly inflated; his estimates go as high as 900 works. However, *Sovremennyi Mir* 5 (1909): 93, section 2, reports that "The Impressionists" had 190 works, and this is confirmed by the exhibition catalogue.

20. "Wreath-Stephanos" closed 8 April; "The Impressionists" opened at the end of April or the beginning of May. "Wreath-Stephanos" presented 78 works *(Sovremennyi Mir* 5 (1909): 93, section 2). The other three painters were A. Gaush, A. Exter, and L. Baranov.

21. Vladimir Baranoff-Rossine, born in Kherson in 1888, attended the Academy of Arts in St. Petersburg, later emigrated to Paris.

22. Drier, *Burliuk:* 50.

23. Kamenskii, *Ego-moia biografiaa velikogo futurista* (M, 1918): 96. See also N. Khardzhiev, "Maiakovskii i zhivopis'," in *Maiakovskii, materialy i issledovaniia* (M, 1940): 348. (In further citations this essay will be referred to with the designation 'I'.)

24. Alexei Kruchenykh, *15 let russkogo futurizma,* (M, 1928): 57-58. Kruchenykh's biting depictions of the elite of his native Kherson were soon to be published in two volumes. *Ves' Kherson. V karikaturakh, sharzhakh i portretakh* Vyp. 1, 2 (Kherson, 1910). When Burliuk's "Wreath-Stephanos" went to Kherson in the fall of 1909, Kruchenykh wrote a review for *Rodnoi krai* (6 September). Khardzhiev, "Maiakovskii i zhivopis'," *Poeticheskaia kul'tura Maiakovskogo* (M, 1970): 312. (In further citations this essay will be referred to with the designation 'II'.)

25. Kamenskii, *Put':* 107. See also Matiushin's memoirs in *K istorii russkogo avangarda,* N. Khardzhiev, ed. (Stockholm, 1976): 140-41.

26. Matiushin was a pupil at the Moscow Conservatory from 1876 to 1881.

27. In his memoirs Matiushin gives some biographical information about Guro. Born in St. Petersburg, Guro grew up in Pskov Province. Her father's father was a French immigrant who had fled revolutionary activity in 1793. Her mother's father was Mikhail Chistiakov, a well known pedagogue and children's writer. He published the *Children's Journal* from 1851-1865, and taught at Moscow University. Guro's mother was also gifted in art, although she did not work at it professionally. *K istorii russkogo avangarda:* 135-36. According to N.I. Khardzhiev, Matiushin was the illegitimate son of a former serf. (Vladimir Markov, in *Russian Futurism* (Berkeley, 1968): 14, reports rumors that Guro was also illegitimate—the daughter of the Emperor.) He entered the Court Orchestra in December 1882, and left it in 1913 upon the death of his wife.

28. "Ranniaia vesna" in *Sbornik molodykh pisatelei*, (SP, 1905) "Pered vesnoi" in *Schast'e* 3 (SP, 1906).

29. In February 1909. *Sharmanka* contained stories, plays and verse by Guro. She also designed the cover and did some of the drawings (others were done by N. Liubavina). *Sharmanka* also contained Matiushin's first musical composition for Guro's play "Harlequin."

30. G. Tasteven, "Impressionizm i novyia iskaniia" in *Zolotoe Runo* 7-9 (1908): XVII. After spending some time in Paris, Tasteven came to the conclusion that Futurism was also an expression of the pervasive idealism which he found characteristic of the modern age. He expounded these views in *Futurizm; na puti k novomu simvolizmu, [Futurism; on the way to the new symbolism]* (M, 1914).

31. "Notes d'un peintre" appeared in no. 6 (1909); "De Gauguin et de Van Gogh" in nos. 5 and 6 (1909).

32. "Salon 1909" a review in *Luch sveta* 1 (15 January 1909): 5. This weekly publication, which had only two issues, was published by Belkov. Kamensky was an editor.

33. N. Kul'bin, *Svobodnaia muzyka. Primenenie novoi teorii khudozhestvennago tvorchestva k muzyke* (SP, 1909). Although published as 1909, the essay itself carries a 1910 date.

   Kul'bin, *Die Freie musik. Die Anwendung der neuen Theorie der Kunstlichen Schaffung zur Musik.* (SP, 1910).

   Koulbine, *La musique libre. Application à la musique de la nouvelle theorie de la creation artistique.* (SP, 1910).

   Another publication, this time a "musical anthology" also called *Free Music* was published early in 1911. It had 33 pages.

34. Studiia impressionistov, N.I. Kul'bin, ed. (SP, 1910), 127 pages. The illustrations included work by E.P. Vashchenko, L.F. Shmit-Ryzhova, A.A. Andreev-Dunichev, N.M. Siniagin, and A.A. Nikolaev.

35. Georgii Ivanov, *Peterburgskie zimy* (NY, 1952): 32.

36. Matiushin's memoirs published in *K istorii russkogo avangarda*, N. Khardzhiev, ed. (Stockholm, 1976), 141.

37. L.F. D'iakonitsyn, *Ideinye protivorechiia v estetike russkoi zhivopisi kontsa 19-nachala 20 vv.* (Perm, 1966): 178. From the archives of the Russian Museum, f. 121, d. 2, 1.21.

38. N. Khardzhiev, "Maiakovskii i zhivopis'," I: 357.

39. Ian Frantsevish Tsionglinskii (1858-1912) had studied at the St. Petersburg Academy of Arts (1879-1885) and in Paris, where he was drawn to Impressionism. He was a member of the Union of Russian Artists and taught at the Academy and in his own studio, where he was influential for many young painters.

40. "Soiuz molodezhy" in *Zolotoe Runo* 11/12 (1909): 101. The lavish "Salon" exhibition of *The Golden Fleece* (its second such exhibit) had taken place just a few weeks previously. (This issue of *The Golden Fleece* was published in April 1910.)

41. *Treugol'nik, katalog* (SP, 1910): 22. The exhibition opened on 19 March at No. 1 Nevsky Prospect and closed on 4 April. The Triangle group had had a slightly earlier exhibition in Vilna (December 1909-January 1910), and "Wreath" had had a show in Saint Petersburg in March of 1909 and in Kherson the following September.

42. L.F. D'iakonitsyn, *Protivorechiia* ... : 155. D'iakonitsyn cites "U impressionistov," N.B.B. (N. Breshko-Breshovskii) in *Birzhovye Vedomosti* 26 March 1911. The year here must be a misprint.

43. "The Triangle" displayed drawings and autographs by A. Pushkin, A. Chekhov, Lev and Aleksei Tolstoy, M. Gorky, A. Blok, L. Andreev, V. Meyerhold, V. Nemirovich-Danchenko, and others, "not only for the elucidation of questions of art, but also for the enjoyment of writers' paintings as works of art." *Apollo* found such an idea "ridiculous" and proceeded to make it so by suggesting "a concert of sculptors, a ballet by architects, monuments by musicians." "Such an exhibition," it scolded Kulbin, "even if it has some interest for the psychologist, is completely out of place next to works of art ..." "N.V.," *Apollon* 7 (April 1910): 24-30.

44. Benois' "Art Letters" appeared in the following issues of *Rech'*: 26 February, no. 56; 5 March, no. 62; 13 March, no. 70; 19 March, no. 76; 26 March, no. 83; V.P. Lapshin, *Soiuz russkikh khudozhnikov* (L, 1974): 228.

45. V.P. Lapshin: 76-83. See also D'iakonitsyn: 144-46.

46. The letter is kept in the archives of the Russian Museum. Excerpts from it are quoted in both D'iakonitsyn, *Protivorechiia:* 146, and Khardzhiev, "Maiakovskii i zhivopis'," II: 311-12. Pieced together from these two sources which differ slightly, the letter appears to read as follows: "What colossal damage, which is difficult to correct, you are doing, discrediting the young Russian art in the eyes of the gullible and trusting public (calling Yakulov, Larionov, Pavel Kuznetsov, mad, etc.) and extolling Petrov-Vodkin, Serebriakova and Lvov. Really these three are unrelated to the 'new art'; they don't present new forms. Larionov is valuable, he moves indefatigably from year to year to the left, to forms ever less bourgeois and more refined, the same with Pavel Kuznetsov. . . . Everyone is against us young people. . . . Even the police are against us; they don't permit us even one place (here it is already two months). . . . Everyone is against us; I, for example, and Vladimir Burliuk and G. Yakulov and others can't exhibit anywhere, and there is nothing to comfort myself with next year, for nothing will change; the banality of Vodkin and Churlionis will always be nicer and more accessible. . . . Don't even you make it hard for us! Be kind, be wary! You have the satisfaction of prosperity. I have, perhaps, the bared teeth of a beast at bay."

47. "Po povodu 'khudozhestvennykh pisem' G-na A. Benua," *Zolotoe Runo* 11/12 (1909): 90-93.

48. *K istorii russkogo avangarda:* 141.

49. Alexander Mitrofanovich Gorodetsky was a poet and sometime painter. It is interesting that this younger brother of the future founder of Acmeism, Sergei Gorodetsky, (in 1912 he published the "Acmeist Manifesto" with N.S. Gumilev) was a participant (although he contributed only one poem) in the first literary publication of the Cubo-Futurists. Both brothers were friends of Kulbin and Sergei had exhibited in "The Triangle."

50. About S. Masoedov, Matiushin says: "[At our apartment] on Litseiskaia St. there used to be S. Masoedov, a teacher of mathematics, an original mind. He used to tell us that in their family, all the Masoedovs spoke to each other in their own language which they invented, and this alone made him a necessary participant in the new art." *K istorii russkogo avangarda:* 143.

51. The description of *Sadok sudei* as a "bomb" is used in the accounts of both Matiushin and Kamensky.

52. *K istorii:* 143.

53. *Put':* 113.

54. *Put':* 114-15.

55. *K istorii:* 143.

56. Ibid.

57. Khardzhiev, "Maiakovskii i zhivopis'," II: 12. The letter is in the archives of the Tretiakov Gallery.

58. "Pchely i osy" in *Apollon* 12 (1910): 57-8.

59. *K istorii:* 143.

60. P. Buzzi, "Poeziia, teatr, muzyka v Italii," *Apollon* 5 (1910): 1-2, section 2. P. Buzzi, "Pis'ma iz Italii" *Apollon* 9 (1910): 14-18, section 2. V. Sh. "Futuristicheskiia dramy na florentiiskoi stsene," *Apollon* 9 (1910): 18-20, section 2. M. Kuzmin, "Futuristy," *Apollon* 9 (1910): 20-21, section 2.

61. *Gagry, Zhukevara Ravine; Gagry, Stones; Gagry, Poplar; Sukhumi, From Cherniavskii Mountain.*

62. Izdebsky's exhibition was called "The International Exhibition of Paintings, Sculpture, Graphics and Drawing." It was in Odessa, 4 Dec. 1909–24 Jan. 1910; in Kiev, 12 Feb.–14 March; Petersburg, 19 April–25 May and Riga, 12 June–7 July. *Salon 2* catalogue: 35.

63. Izdebsky did exceptionally well in assembling the French modernists; of the twenty-one artists shown in the "Exposition du Cercle de l'Art Modern" held in LeHavre in June 1908, fifteen were represented in the "Salon." For a discussion of Expressionism and a history of the term, see D.E. Gordon, "On the Origin of the Word 'Expressionism'," in *Warburg and Courtauld Institute Journal* 29, (1966): 368-85. This study will follow Gordon's use of the word.

64. D. Robbins, "From Symbolism to Cubism," *Art Journal* 23 (1963-64), no. 2: 115-16.

65. The first Futurist Manifesto was published by F.T. Marinetti on 20 Feb. 1909 (n.s.). Balla signed the "Manifesto of the Futurist Painters" and "Futurist Painting: Technical Manifesto," both published in the time between the "Salon's" opening in Odessa and its arrival in St. Petersburg. He was the only signatory of these documents represented in the "Salon."

66. In 1910 at the second exhibition of the New Artists Federation several of the French participants in "Salon," Braque, Van Dongen, Rouault, and Vlaminck, were included as "guests." Le Fauconnier had become a member. Hans K. Roethel, *The Blue Rider* (NY, 1971): 19.

67. *Salon. Katalog internatsional'noi vystavki kartin, skul'ptury, graviury i risunkov. 1909-1910.*

68. Archive of the Russian Museum. Quoted by N. Khardzhiev in "Maiakovskii i zhivopis' " II: 31.

69. A. Rostislavov, "Khudozhestvennaia zhizn' Peterburga," *Apollon* 8 (1910): 47. See also N. Khardzhiev, "Maiakovskii i zhivopis'," II: 31. Although the Burliuks were added to the exhibition late, they were some of its few exhibitors who managed to sell something. See *Salon 2* catalogue: 35.

70. "O Salone Izdebskago" *Zolotoe Runo* 11/12 (1909): 95.

71. A. Rostislavov mentioned this in the review for *Apollon*. See note 69.

72. Benedikt Livshits, *Polutoraglazyi strelets* (L, 1933): 17-18. This memoir has recently appeared in an English translation by John E. Bowlt: Benedikt Livshits, *The One and a Half-Eyed Archer* (Newtonville, Mass., 1977).

73. D. Burliuk, "Our Friendship with W.W. Kandinsky," *Color and Rhyme* 51/52: 9; M. Lentulova, *Khudozhnik Aristarkh Lentulov* (M, 1969): 17.

74. Khardzhiev, "Maiakovskii i zhivopis' " I: 357.

75. M. Lentulova: 32.

76. Among the Russians at the "Jack of Diamonds" who had been to Paris were Exter, Konchalovsky, Morgunov, the Burliuks, Mashkov, Larionov and Goncharova. Lentulov went to study in Paris with Le Fauconnier after the exhibition. Grabar', *Istoriia russkogo iskusstva:* 117.

77. Relatively little is known about Malevich's personal life. He was born 26 February 1878 of Ludvika Alexandrovna and Severin Malevich, a manager at the Tereshtchenko sugar refinery near Kiev. Malevich had three brothers, Boleslav, Antoni, and Mechislav, and two sisters; the family spoke Polish at home. (When Malevich applied for a visa to Paris in 1926 he listed his nationality as "Polish.")

   His first marriage, in Moscow, was to Kazimira Zgleitz by whom he had a daughter, Galina, now dead. The marriage was dissolved in 1909. Malevich's second wife, Sofia

Mikhailovna Rafalovich, died of tuberculosis; a daughter from the marriage, Una, now lives in Central Asia. His third wife lives in Leningrad. Two partial autobiographies have been published: the shorter dates from 1918 and appears in English as "1/42. Notes" in K.S. Malevich, *Essays on Art: 1915-1933:* II (London, 1969): 147-54. The initial chapters (32 ms. pages) of a projected longer treatment were written in 1933 and annotated and published by N. Khardzhiev as "Detstvo i junost Kazimira Malevicha; glavy iz autobiografii khudozhnika" in *K istorii russkogo avangarda* (Stockholm, 1976): 85-127. These works relate Malevich's vivid memories of an unfettered childhood in the provincial towns of Parkhomovka, Belopol'e and Volchok, his first attempts at painting and his work as a clerk for the Moscow-Kursk railroad to finance his move to Moscow in 1904. There he lived in a communal house with other young artists and attended Rerberg's studio. For several summers he continued to return to Kursk.

78. Anderson, *Malevich:* 161.

79. Ibid.

80. For example, Larionov's *The Baker* (1909) and *Portrait of a Man* (1910).

81. The final issue of *The Golden Fleece* was published in April 1910.

82. There were fifteen Russian painters common to both exhibitions.

83. As mentioned above, Dydyshko had appeared in both the Triangle and Wreath sections of "The Triangle."

This seems to be the first time Tatlin appears with the avant-garde as an exhibitor (although Kamensky, perhaps erroneously, reported him in the crowds at "Modern Trends" in 1908). Tatlin appears next at the "Union of Youth" exhibit which opened in St. Petersburg in April 1911; he is listed there as a "Moscow" painter. Since he had known Larionov for several years already, it is notable that he was not in the "Jack of Diamonds." Possibly this is because at the time he was enrolled at the Moscow School of Painting, Sculpture and Architecture (after having graduated the preceding April from the Penza Art School), and the school's administration frowned on such activities.

From the confused account by David Burliuk in *Color and Rhyme* 51/52: 9, it appears he was introduced to Kandinsky by Izdebsky during the "Salon 2" exhibition. He reports being asked by Kandinsky at this time for an article about the "Russian Fauves," although Kandinsky could not have had it in mind for the *Blue Rider Almanac* (since his letters attest that the idea for the *Almanac* originated only in the spring of 1911). Khardzhiev, in "Maiakovskii i zhivopis'," II: 312, reports that Burliuk's article for *The Blue Rider* was originally much longer, was called "A Word to Russian Artists (Concerning the Congress)," and was written in 1911. Burliuk also had a piece in the catalogue for "Neue Kunstlervereinigung" ("New Artists Federation"), 1910/1911. This article, however, may have come about through Izdebsky (whom Burliuk had known since his stay in Munich in 1902).

Perhaps Kulbin, too, met Kandinsky at this time. A year later Kandinsky was to entrust his "Concerning the Spiritual in Art" (a version of which appeared as "Content and Form" in the *Salon 2* catalogue) to Kulbin to read at the All Russian Congress of Artists. (See below.)

84. Vladimir Izdebskii, "Griadushchii gorod" in the catalogue, *Salon 2* (Odessa, 1910): 12.

85. V. Kandinskii, "Soderzhanie i forma," *Salon 2:* 14-16; Arnol'd Shenberg, "Paralleli v oktavakh i kvintakh," *Salon 2:* 16-18.

86. See *Trudy vserossiiskogo s'ezda khudozhnikov v Petrograde, Dekabr' 1911-Ianvar';* *1912* I (Petrograd, 1914).

87. *Trudy:* 36.

88. *Trudy:* 38, 39.

89. *Trudy:* 41-45.

90. Kandinsky always kept himself well informed about artistic ideas and events in Russia. He corresponded with Kulbin from about the summer of 1910 and met many of the Moscow avant-garde when he visited there in October of the same year. In November he went to Odessa in preparation for "Salon 2." He sent Kulbin a copy of "Das Geistige in der Kunst" on 12 December 1911 (probably new style), asking him to read it at the Congress. In January he asked Kulbin for any notices or reviews of the paper and was quite anxious for the Russian publication. Archives of the Russian Museum f. 134, ed. khr. 35.

91. "Printsipy novago iskusstva," *Soiuz molodezhi* I (April, 1912): 5-14; II (June, 1912): 5-18. An English translation appears in *Russian Art of the Avant-Garde: Theory and Criticism,* John E. Bowlt, ed. (NY, 1976): 23-38.

92. N. Khardzhiev, "Maiakovskii i zhivopis'," II: 13.

93. N. Khardzhiev, "Maiakovskii i zhivopis'," II: 14.

94. Most of the literary manifestos are reprinted in *Manifesty i programmy russkikh futuris-tov,* V. Markov, ed., Munich, 1967. A French translation of many manifestos is given in *Manifestes Futuristes Russes* (Paris, 1971) by Leon Robel.

Chapter 2

1. The date of incorporation is given by Burliuk as "summer 1911" (*Color and Rhyme* 51/52: 9); Khardzhiev places it at the "end of 1911" ("Maiakovskii i zhivopis'," I: 357).

2. D. Burliuk, "Our Friendship with W.W. Kandinsky," *Color and Rhyme* 51/52:9.

3. M. Lentulova: 33.

4. Khardzhiev, "Maiakovskii i zhivopis'," I: 358.

5. The "First Exhibition of the Editors of the *Blue Rider*" opened in Munich on 18 December 1911 (n.s.); both Vladimir and David Burliuk were represented in it. The "Second Exhibition of the Editors of the *Blue Rider*" opened either in February 1912, according to Gordon in *Modern Art Exhibitions 1900-1916* (Munich, 1974) II: 548, or in March, according to Klaus Lankheit in *The Blaue Reiter Almanac* (NY, 1974): 14. This was an

exhibit of drawings, watercolors and graphics. The Burliuks did not participate, but Larionov, Goncharova and Malevich did. At the "First German Fall Salon" which opened 20 September 1913, the Russian participants included Vladimir and David Burliuk, Chagall, Goncharova, Larionov, Yakulov, and Kulbin.

6. Livshits gives 25 January as the opening date. *Polutoraglazyi:* 65.

7. Kandinsky's relationship with The New Artists Federation had been worsening since summer. The final break came on 2 December 1911 (n.s.).

8. According to Livshits, *Polutoraglazyi:* 65.

9. Kandinsky had originally intended to return to Russia in the spring of 1912. In a letter of 13 January 1912 (n.s.) to Kulbin, he promises definitely to visit him in St. Petersburg at that time. (Archives of the Russian Museum f. 134, ed. khr. 35, s. 21). The trip, however, was repeatedly postponed. On 9 June 1912, just after his return from a trip abroad, Burliuk wrote to Kulbin about the coming season: "V.V. Kandinsky will be in Moscow in the winter; get ready for winter. . . ." Khardzhiev, "Maiakovskii i zhivopis'," II: 13. Kandinsky seems to corroborate this on 24 June in a letter to F.A. Gartman: "Burliuk and Konchalovsky were here. . . . *Entre nous:* Burliuk made various propositions to me. Later in the fall I hope to participate personally in various enterprises in Moscow." Ibid: 18. (The recipient of the letter is the Russian composer Foma Aleksandrovich Gartman, known variously as Thomas de Hartmann and Thomas von Hartmann, who before 1914 lived periodically in Munich. A student of the correlation of music and movement, he composed the music for Kandinsky's *The Yellow Sound.)* Kandinsky finally did arrive in Moscow in October.

10. The comparison between work of recognized artists and photographs so enraged the critics (see, for example, Essem (Sergei Makovsky), in *Apollon* 2 (1913): 56) that it became a favorite rhetorical device of the young artists. Kulbin once created a major scandal by comparing Konstantin Somov's work with illustrations from a ladies' magazine.

11. A very complete account of the evening (at variance, however, with records about several minor points) may be found in Livshits, *Polutoraglazyi:* 65ff.

12. An excerpt from her letter to *Stolichnaia molva* and published 20 February 1912 in issue no. 230 is quoted by Khardzhiev, "Maiakovskii i zhivopis' " I: 539. Her complete letter to *Russkoe slovo* is given (in French) in Tatiana Loguine, *Goncharova et Larionov* (Paris, 1971): 21-23.

13. A detailed description of the works presented in "The Ass's Tail" may be found in C. Gray, *The Great Experiment 1883-1922* (NY, 1962): 122ff. The title of the work by Chagall is *Death (Smert'),* but since there is no work with exactly this title listed in Chagall catalogues, it is not possible to ascertain exactly which painting appeared. (A classified catalogue of the works of Chagall may be found in Franz Meyer, *Marc Chagall: Life and Work* (NY, 1965?): 745-63.) Most probably it was one of a series depicting the stages of life done in St. Petersburg in 1910. The Union of Youth participated in "The Ass's Tail" as a separate section (apparently with a separate catalogue or perhaps even with none at all). This is the first and only time the Union appeared in Moscow, and their friendly association with The Ass's Tail helps to explain Larionov's reaction when it was Burliuk's group a year later who contracted a formal association with the

Union. The Union participants in "The Ass's Tail" were: Varvarova, Dydyshko, Zel'-manova, Kurchaninova, L'vov, Nagubnikov, Novodvorskaia, Potinaka, Rozanova, Spandikov, Shkol'nik, Shleifer, Iasenskii, Filonov, and Markov.

14. Livshits, *Polutoraglazyi:* 90.

15. Malevich's work is entitled *Bauernkopf (Peasant's Head)* in the catalogue. Gordon, *Modern Art Exhibitions* II: 549.

16. Khardzhiev quotes a few sentences on this topic from Malevich's unpublished biography in "Maiakovskii i zhivopis'," I: 359.

17. Ia. Tugendkhol'd, *Apollon* 1 (1913): 41. The phrase is "bubnovye valety i khvosty."

18. *Photographic Study from Nature of a City Street, Momentary Photograph, Photographic Study of Melted Snow in Spring.* Gordon, *Modern Art Exhibitions* II: 564.

19. Larionov's Theory of Rayism is given in the manifesto "Luchisty; budushchiki" ("Rayists and Future People") and his article "Luchistaia zhivopis' " ("Rayist Painting") both published in *Oslinyi khvost i mishen'* (M, 1913). An English translation may be found in *Russian Art of the Avant- Garde:* 87-100.

20. Zdanevich, the son of a French teacher, had been in France in 1912. In 1913, under the name of Eli Eganbyuri, he published *Nataliia Goncharova, Mikhail Larionov,* a book which remains the best source for the early lives and work of these painters.

21. On Zdanevich's first lecture see N. Khardzhiev, "Maiakovskii i zhivopis'," I: 371. For the second: *Rech'* (9 April 1913); and S. Khudakov "Literatura, khudozhestvennaia kritika, disputy i doklady" in *Osliny khvost i mishen'.*

22. "Doklad o futurizme," *Rech'* (9 April 1913).

23. Mikhail Larionov, Ilia Zdanevich, "Pochemu my raskrashivaemsia. Manifest futuristov," *Argus* (Dec. 1913): 114-18. "Why We Paint Ourselves," *Russian Art of the Avant-Garde,* 80-83.

24. Klaus Lankheit, "A History of the Almanac" in *The Blaue Reiter Almanac,* Klaus Lankheit, ed. (NY, 1974): 31.

25. At the "Union of Youth" exhibition which opened on 4 December 1912 in St. Petersburg. This exhibition directly foreshadowed the most important revelations of "Target," not only in presenting Malevich's volumetric figures such as *Women in the Field* and *Portrait of Ivan Kliunkov* (both of which reappeared in "Target"), but also in showing Larionov's new *Rayist Sausage and Mackerel.* The general interest in the discontinuity of the painted image inspired by Analytical Cubism and Futurism may be deduced from Burliuk's didactic titles such as *Moments of Decomposition of the Planes and Elements of Wind and Evening, Introduced into a Scene Depicting the Edge of the Sea from Four Points of View,* or *Light-lines Conceptualized According to the Assyrian Method and the Principle of Flowing Color.* At the time of this exhibition Larionov and his group were loosely allied with the "Union." See note 13 above.

26. For Malevich's lecture see N. Khardzhiev, "Maiakovskii i zhivopis'," I: 365, 366.

27. "Oslinyi khvost i mishen'," *Oslinyi khvost i mishen':* 65, 72.

28. *K istorii* . . . : 146.

29. A. Kruchenykh, *15 let russkogo futurizma* (M, 1928): 58.

30. Khardzhiev, "Maiakovskii i zhivopis'," II: 12.

31. A. Kruchenykh i V. Khlebnikov, *Igra v adu* (M, 1912); Goncharova, ill.

    A. Kruchenykh, *Starinnaia liubov* (M, 1912); Larionov, ill.

    A. Kruchenykh i V. Khlebnikov, *Mirskontsa* (M, 1912); Larionov, Goncharova, Tatlin, Rogovin, ill.

    A. Kruchenykh, *Poluzhivoi* (M, 1913); Larionov, ill.

    A. Kruchenykh, *Dve poemy. Pustynniki. Pustynnitsa* (M, 1913); Goncharova, ill.

    A. Kruchenykh, *Pomada* (M, 1913); Larionov, ill.

32. The designation "Cubo-Futurists" was adopted by the Hyleans and their friends in 1913.

33. "Samotsennoe (samovitoe), Slovo," in the manifesto "Poshchechina obshchestvennomu vkusu," see (a) below. The manifesto is signed by D. Burliuk, Kruchenykh, Mayakovsky, and Khlebnikov. Reprinted in *Manifesty i programmy russkikh futuristov,* V. Markov, ed. (Munich, 1967): 50.

    Kruchenykh's most important theoretical statements from this period are contained in:

    a) "Poshchechina obshchestvennomu vkusu," *Poshchechina obshchestvennomu vkusu* (M, 1912); reprinted in *Manifesty i programmy russkikh futuristov:* 50-51.

    b) An untitled manifesto published in *Sadok Sudei* II (SP, 1913). In addition to Kruchenykh, it was signed by D. Burliuk, Guro, N. Burliuk, Mayakovsky, Nizen, Khlebnikov, and Livshits. Reprinted in *Manifesty:* 51-53.

    c) A. Kruchenykh, V. Khlebnikov, *Slovo kak takovoe* (M, 1913); reprinted in *Manifesty:* 53-58.

    d) *Deklaratsiia slova, kak takovogo* (SP, 1913); reprinted in *Manifesty:* 63-64.

    e) "Novye puti slova," A. Kruchenykh, V. Khlebnikov, E. Guro, *Troe* (SP, 1913); reprinted in *Manifesty:* 64-73.

    f) "Pervyi Vserossiiskii s'ezd baiachei budushchego," *Za 7 dnei* 28/122 (SP, 1913): 605-6.

Short statements and polemical and critical pieces may be found in half a dozen additional publications.

34. Matiushin's culminating works on these topics are: *Zakonomernost' izmeniaemosti tsvetochnykh sochetanii* (M, 1932) and *Opyt khudozhnika novoi mery.* The latter has never been published in Russian. A Ukrainian version, "Sproba novogo vidchuttia prostoroni" appeared in *Novaia generatsiia* 11 (1928): 311-22.

35. In "New Ways of the Word" and *The Word as Such,* for example.

36. In "Pervyi vserossiiskii s'ezd baiachei budushchego" Kruchenykh, Matiushin, and Malevich promised to "destroy the antiquated movement of thought according to the law of causality, the toothless, common sense, the 'symmetrical logic' wandering about in the blue shadows of Symbolism. . . ." *Za 7 Dnei* 28/122 (SP, 1913): 605-6. See also Chapter 3 of this study.

37. "Svobodnoe iskusstvo, kak osnova zhizni," *Studiia impressionistov,* N.I. Kulbin, ed. (SP, 1910): 11. Kulbin's theoretical statements about art are contained in:

a) *Svobodnaia muzyka* (SP, 1909); also published in French and German. An article by the same name appeared in *Studiia impressionistov,* N.I. Kul'bin, ed. (SP, 1910): 15-26.

b) "Svobodnoe iskusstvo, kak osnova zhizni," *Studiia impressionistov:* 3-14.

c) Statement (untitled) in the catalogue *Salon 2* (Odessa, 1910-1911): 19.

d) "Garmoniia, dissonans i tesnyia sochetaniia v iskusstve i zhizni," *Trudy Vserossiiskogo s'ezda khudozhnikov v Petrograde. Dekabr', 1911 – Ianvar', 1912* 1 (P, 1914): 35-40.

e) *Chto est' slovo (II deklaratsiia slova kak takogo)* (SP, 1914). Republished in *Gramoty i deklaratsii russkikh futuristov* (SP, 1914): n.p.

f) "Novyi tsik slova," *Gramoty:* n.p.

g) "Kubizm," *Strelets,* A. Belenson, ed., 1 (P, 1915): 197-216.

38. "Svobodnoe iskusstvo, kak osnova zhizni": 7.

39. *Manifesty:* 64.

40. Waldemars Matvejs (Vladimir Markov), "Printsipy novago iskusstva," *Soiuz molodezhi,* 2: 15.

41. "Pervyi vserossiiskii s'ezd baiachei budushchego": 605.

42. P.D. Uspenskii, *Chetvertoe izmerenie, Opyt izsledovaniia oblasti neizmerimago* (SP, 1909); *Tertium organum, Kliuch k zagadkam mira* (SP, 1911). Somewhat later Uspenskii translated and introduced Hinton's *Vospitanie voobrazheniia* (P, 1915), and Carpenter's *Liubov' i smert'* (P, 1915). Another Russian translation of Hinton, *Chetvertoe izmerenie i era novoi mysli,* was published early in 1915.

43. Charles Howard Hinton, *A New Era of Thought* (London, 1888), *The Fourth Dimension* (NY, 1904).

44. Petr Uspenskii, *Tertium Organum,* as quoted by Matiushin in "O Knige Metsanzhe-Gleza 'Du Cubisme'," *Soiuz Molodezhi* 3 (March, 1913): 25, 28.

45. Manifesto in *Sadok sudei II* (SP, February, 1913). Reprinted in *Manifesty:* 52. The manifesto was signed by David and Nikolai Burliuk, Guro, Mayakovsky, Ekaterina Nizen, Khlebnikov, Livshits and Kruchenykh.

46. In Metzinger "Note sur la peinture," *Pan* (October/November 1910): 650.

47. For an exhaustive study of modern art and ideas of the fourth dimension, see Linda Henderson, *The Artist, "The Fourth Dimension" and Non-Euclidean Geometry 1900-1930: A Romance of Many Dimensions,* unpublished Ph.D. dissertation, (Yale University, 1975).

48. Sergei Makovskii, " 'Novoe' iskusstvo i 'chertvertoe izmerenie'," *Apollon* 7 (1913): 57.

49. A. Kruchenykh, K. Malevich, I. Kliun, *Tainye proroki akademikov* (M., 1916) translated as "Secret Vices of the Academicians" in Kazimir Malevich, *Essays on Art* I, Troels Andersen, ed. (London, 1968): 17.

50. The title refers to Khlebnikov, Guro and Kruchenykh.

51. *Troe* (SP, 1913): 3.

52. Edward Fry, *Cubism* (NY, 1966): 116.

53. *Soiuz molodezhi* 3 (SP, 1913): 5.

54. Ibid.

55. A. Gleizes, J. Metzinger, *Du Cubisme* (Paris, 1962), as translated in R.L. Herbert, *Modern Artists on Art* (Englewood, 1964): 13.

56. *Manifesty:* 68, 72.

57. *Manifesty:* 64.

58. *Manifesty:* 68.

59. "Novye puti slova," in *Manifesty:* 71.

60. "Novye puti slova," in *Manifesty:* 72.

Chapter 3

1. Velimir Khlebnikov, *Neizdanny proizvedeniia,* N. Khardzhiev and T. Grits, eds. (M, 1940): 366.

2. *Sobranie proizvedenii Velimira Khlebnikova,* N. Stepanov, ed. (L, 1933): 298-99. The date of this letter is here incorrect. See Khlebnikov, *Neizdannye proizvedeniia:* 473.

3. Aleksei Kruchenykh, "O knigakh baiachei" in *Futuristy: Pervyi zhurnal russkikh futuristov* (M, 1914), cited in Maiakovskii, *Polnoe Sobranie Sochinenii,* 1, V. Trenin and N. Khardzhiev, eds. (M, 1935):392.

4. *Za 7 dnei* no. 28, pt. 122: 605-6. "The time of slaps" refers to "A Slap in the Face of Public Taste," a Futurist manifesto of December 1912, signed by Khlebnikov, Kruchenykh, Burliuk and Mayakovsky. "We intend to arm the world against us" is very similar to a line in the opening scene of *Victory Over the Sun.*

5. From a letter cited in Mayakovskii, *Polnoe Sobranie Sochinenii* 1: 391.

6. The most complete description of the performance of *Victory Over the Sun* is given in K. Tomashevskii, "Vladimir Maiakovsky," in *Teatr* 4 (1938): 137-50.

7. *Pobeda nad solntsem: Opera v 2 deimakh 6 kartinakh,* muzyka M.V. Matiushina, dekoratsii Kaz. S. Malevicha, prolog Viktor Khlebnikova (SP, 1914). An English translation by Ewa Bartos and Victoria Nes Kirby is given in *The Drama Review,* 15/4 (Fall, 1971): 106-24.

8. The limited scope of the characters and their apparent awareness of the audience sometimes caused contemporary critics to take the Futurist productions for Evreinov-inspired monodramas.

9. M. Matiushin, "Futurizm v Peterburge," *Futuristy. Pervy i zhurnal russkikh futuristov* 1-2 (M, 1914): 156.

10. *Pobeda nad soltsem:* 15.

11. Ibid.: 14.

12. Vladimir Maiakovskii, *Vladimir Maiakovskii, tragediia,* in V.V. Maiakovskii, *Sobranie sochinenii v 8 tomakh,* I: 38.

13. *Pobeda:* 12.

14. Ibid.: 14.

15. Ibid.: 15.

16. Ibid.: 16.

17. Ibid.: 18.

18. Ibid.: 7.

19. Ibid.: 17.

20. Ibid.: 19.

21. Ibid.: 20.

22. Ibid.: 21.

23. Ibid.: 23.

24. Ibid.: 19.

25. *Vladimir Maiakovskii:* 37, 44.

26. Ibid.: 42.

27. *Pobeda:* 19.

28. Ibid.: 20.

29. These sketches are located in the Leningrad Theatrical Museum.

30. Kruchenykh's letter to Matiushin is given in "A.E. Kruchenykh, pis'ma k M.V. Matiu-shinu," publikatsiia B.N. Kapeliush in *Ezhegodnik rukopisnogo otdela Pushkinskogo doma na 1974 god* (L, 1976): 171. For descriptions of the costumes see extracts from Kruchenykh, "Nash vykhod," and Matiushin's interview in *Den'*, both quoted in Camilla Gray, *The Great Experiment* (NY, 1962): 308, and K. Tomashevskii, "Vladimir Maya-kovskii," in *Teatr* 4 (1938): 140-41. The two contemporary newspaper photographs are reproduced by Troels Andersen in K.S. Malevich, *The Artist, Infinity, Suprematism* (Copenhagen, 1978): 17-18.

31. Benedikt Livshits, *Polutoraglazyi strelets* (L, 1933): 189.

32. Ibid.: 187-88.

33. These geometrical shapes, along with the projectors, are also mentioned in Kruchenykh's memoirs, quoted in Gray, *The Great Experiment:* 308. They can be seen in the photo-graphs reproduced by Andersen. See note 30 above.

34. Ibid.: 308.

35. This painting *(Musical Instrument/Lamp)* has much in common with both the sketch for the house set and the set for act one, scene three.

36. T. Andersen, *Malevich* (Amsterdam, 1970): 103.

37. Kazimir Malevich, *Ot kubizma k suprematizmu. Novyi zhivopisnyi realizm.* (P, 1916). See Appendix.

38. *Výtvarné Uměni* 8/9 (1967): 380-81.

39. *Suprematist Painting* (1917), *Suprematist Painting* (1917-1918) (Andersen nos. 61 and 64).

Chapter 4

1. See the account published in *Russkie vedomosti,* 12 November 1913, reprinted in V. Katanian, *Maiakovskii, literaturnaia khronika* (M, 1961): 51-52. Maiakovsky's outline for his talk is given in N. Khardzhiev, "Turne kubo-futuristov 1913-1914" in *Maiakovskii. Materialy i issledovaniia,* V.O. Pertsov and M.I. Serebrianskii, eds. (M, 1940) 417.

2. In later years Marinetti seems to have wished he had visited his Russian colleagues sooner and arranged his memoirs to be ambiguous about just when and how many times he went to Russia. Western scholars have repeatedly fallen into his trap. The mystery is disentangled in Kjeld Bjørnager Jensen, "Marinetti in Russia 1910, 1912, 1913, 1914?" *Scando-Slavica* tomus XV 1969:21.

3. *Russkie vedomosti,* 31 December 1913; cited in Khardzhiev, "Turne kubo-futuristov 1913-1914": 417.

4. Tasteven had met Marinetti by June 1913 and considered him an "extremely nice and charmingly frivolous Italian." The invitation to Russia was extended both in the spring and fall of 1913, and for his lecture in Moscow Tasteven proposed to pay him 300 roubles. Marinetti recounts Tasteven's invitation in his memoirs:

   ". . . Tasteven a small carefully dressed gentleman looking like an important official of some ministry comes over to greet me his blond goatee twitching and his little red Russian eyes sparkling.

   "As director of the lecturer's group in Moscow I have the honor of inviting you to give a series of lectures in the larger Russian cities lectures for which you will be paid whatever you ask with half your fee in advance and traveling expenses do come soon if possible because they're waiting for you anxiously in Saint Petersburg and Moscow" in "The Birth of Russian Futurism Milan, Paris, Moscow, Saint Petersburg," *Marinetti's Writings,* R.W. Flint, ed. (NY, 1971): 345.

5. Marinetti arrived in Russia on 26 January 1914. The most complete account of the vicissitudes of his visits to Moscow and St. Petersburg is given in N.I. Khardzhiev, " 'Veselyi god' Maiakovskogo" in *Vladimir Majakovskij, Memoirs and Essays,* Bengt-Jangfeldt and Nils Ake Nilsson, eds. (Stockholm, 1975): 108-51. For an account in English see V. Markov, *Russian Futurism* (Berkeley, 1968): 147ff.

6. The "Technical Manifesto of Futurist Painting" was published separately by the journal *Poesia* in Milan, 11 April 1910. As mentioned previously, a substantial portion of this was reprinted by *Apollon* in July/August 1910, but seems to have gone unnoticed. A more effective introduction of this manifesto into Russia occurred when it was reprinted in February 1912 in the Bernheim-Jeune exhibition catalogue along with the important "Exhibitors to the Public" statement, and both appeared in the *Union of Youth* journal in April (see Chapter 1). Of great importance to Malevich seems to have been Boccioni's "Technical Manifesto of Futurist Sculpture" of mid-1912. This appears to have gone untranslated into Russian until after Marinetti's visit.

7. See Marinetti's "Words-in-Freedom" in "Destruction of Syntax—Imagination without Strings—Words in Freedom" published in *Lacerba* 15 June 1913. Although Kruchenykh's

theories differ substantially from those of Marinetti, he owes a great deal to this manifesto, published just before the "First All-Russian Congress of Poets of the Future" (see Chapter 3).

8. Illustrations by Malevich appear in *Slovo kak takovoe* (SP, 1913); *Troe* (SP, 1913); *Vozropshchem* (SP, 1913); *Vzorval'* (SP, 1913); *Porosiata* (SP, 1913) and *Igra v adu* (SP, 1914).

9. See Chapter 3.

10. Burliuk's end page drawing for the published version of *Victory Over the Sun* seems to make reference to this painting, as well as to the "Technical Manifesto of Painting."

11. Archives of the Tretiakov Gallery, f. 25, no. 9, l. 7-8, and l. 11-12. Other English translations may be found in Evgenii Kovtun, "Die Entstehung des Suprematismus/The Beginning of Suprematism," in *Von de Fläche zum Raum: Russland 1916-24/From Surface to Space: Russia 1916-24* (Cologne, 1974): 32-47; and K.S. Malevich, *The Artist, Infinity, Suprematism*, IV, Troels Andersen, ed. (Copenhagen, 1978): 203-4.

12. This is evident from Malevich's letters.

13. June 1916. K.S. Malevich, "Pis'ma k M.V. Matiushinu," publikatsiia E.F. Kovtuna in *Ezhegodnik rukopisnogo otdela Pushkinskogo doma na 1974 god.* (L, 1976): 192.

14. K.S. Malevich, "From Cubism and Futurism to Suprematism. The New Realism in Painting" (1916) in *Essays on Art 1915-1933*, I, Troels Andersen, ed. (London, 1969): 32.

15. Ibid.: 33.

16. Ibid.: 38.

17. Ibid.: 31.

18. A. Bergson, *Tvorcheskaia evoliutsiia* (M, 1909); *Vremia i svoboda voli*, s prilozheniem stat'ia "Vvedenie k metafiziku" (M, 1911); *Materiia i pamiat'* (SP, 1911); *Vospriiatie izmenchivosti* (SP, 1912); *Psikhofiziologicheskii paralogizm i snovideniia* (SP, 1913); *Vospominanie nastoiashchago* (SP, 1913); *Intellektual'noe usilie: Zametka o psikhologicheskom proiskhozhdenii nashei very v zakon prichinosti* (SP, 1913); *Sobranie sochinenii*, 5 vols. (SP, 1913-1914).

19. I. Rozenfel'd, "Intuitivizm i futurizm," *Maski* 6 (1913-14): 17-26. This author makes no distinction between Russian and Italian Futurists in his discussion of the influence of Bergson.

20. Many of the Italian manifestos, including Marinetti's first proclamation, Boccioni's "Technical Manifesto of Painting," and Russolo's "The Art of Noises" appeared in Russia almost as soon as they were published in Western Europe. After Marinetti's visit, however, two collections of manifestos were published: *Manifesty ital'ianskogo futurizma. Sobranie manifestov.* Vadim Shershenevich, trans. (M, 1914); and *Futurizm*, by Genrikh Tasteven (M, 1914).

21. B. Livshits, *Polutoraglazyi strelets* (L, 1933): 225.

22. H. Bergson, *The Creative Mind*, trans. M.L. Andisom (NY, 1946): 103; Bergson, *Introduction to Metaphysics*, trans. T.E. Hulme (NY, 1912): 69.

23. Malevich, "From Cubism and Futurism to Suprematism" in *Essays*, I: 19.

24. H. Bergson, *Creative Evolution*, trans. A. Mitchell (NY, 1911): 278-79.

25. Bergson, *Introduction to Metaphysics:* 65.

26. Malevich, "From Cubism and Futurism to Suprematism. The New Realism in Painting." (1916) in *Essays* I: 19.

27. 29 May 1915. K.S. Malevich, "Pis'ma k M.V. Matiushinu" in *Ezhegodnik:* 186. See Chapter 5.

28. *From Cubism to Suprematism* (P, 1916 [1915]); Appendix: 109, 110.

29. Malevich, "From Cubism and Futurism to Suprematism" in *Essays*, I:24-25.

30. Ibid.: 37.

31. See note 20, this chapter, Shershenevich's book is a collection of thirteen manifestos including "The Technical Manifesto of Futurist Sculpture," Carra's "The Painting of Sounds, Noises and Smells" and Marinetti's "The Variety Theater." Tasteven's book has an appendix with five manifestos, three of which are contained in Shershenevich's selection.

32. Umberto Boccioni, "Manifesto tecnico della scultura futurista" in *Gli scritti editi e inediti*, Zeno Birolli, ed. (Milano, 1971): 30.

33. K.S. Malevich, "From Cubism and Futurism . . .": 31, 38.

34. Andersen, *Malevich* (Amsterdam, 1970): 162.

35. Translated into English from *Lacerba* and reprinted in *Futurist Manifestos*, Umbro Apollonio, ed. (NY, 1973): 93.

36. Boccioni, "Dinamismo" in *Pittura e scultura futuristi* in *Gli scritti:* 150.

37. Boccioni, "Noi porremo lo spettatore nel centro del quadro" in *Pittura e scultura futuristi, Gli scritti:* 173.

38. Central State Archives for Literature and Art: f. 134, op. 2, ed. khr. 24, s. 2.

39. See note 47, Chapter 2.

40. M. Matiushin, "O vystavke 'posslednikh futuristov'," in *Ocharovannyi strannik*, al'-manakh vesenii (1916): 17.

Chapter 5

1. The participants in "0-10" were N. Al'tman, K. Boguslavskaia, V. Kamenskii, A. Kirillova, I. Kliun, K. Malevich, M. Men'kov, V. Pestel', L. Popova, I. Puni, O. Rozanova, V. Tatlin, N. Udal'tsova and M. Vasil'eva. Because Malevich and Tatlin were not on friendly terms the exhibition was divided into two separate sections. Several pieces of explanatory literature were available to the public: the catalogue of the entire exhibition, *The Last Futurist Exhibition. "0-10"* (P, 1915), an illustrated booklet of Tatlin's work, a one page statement by Puni and Boguslavskaia, short statements by Malevich, Kliun and Men'kov all on one page, and Malevich's brochure, *From Cubism to Suprematism* (P, 1916 [1915]). The "0-10" catalogue is photoreproduced in H. Berninger and J. Cartier, *Pougny* (Tubingen, 1972): 58-59. The statements of the five artists are given in English in *Russian Art of the Avant-Garde,* John E. Bowlt, ed. (NY, 1976): 110-14. An English translation of Malevich's brochure is appended to the present volume.

2. Malevich also exhibited five works which are not dated in the catalogue and which are grouped under the general designation "Content of the Picture not Known to the Artist." No identification of these works has yet been made, although it is fairly certain they were not Suprematist.

   Tatlin had had previous showings of his reliefs. For five days in May 1914—from the 10th to the 14th—he opened his studio to visitors for two hours each evening. The invitation to this showing called the work "synthetic-static compositions." For an hour each evening during the showing the poet Sergei Podchaevskii (who had also taken part in the "Union of Youth" exhibition the previous November) declaimed his "postzaum" poetry. See Tatlin's invitation to the exhibition, Archives of the Russian Museum: f. 121, ed. khr. 117. no. 61.

3. On 28 November 1914 he wrote to Matiushin, "I am impatiently waiting for the stretchers I ordered so that I can begin my Februaryism," Pushkin House Archive, Leningrad. Quoted after Evgenii Kovtun, "The Beginning of Suprematism," *From Surface to Space: Russia 1916-1924,* exhibition catalogue, Galerie Gmurzynska, (Cologne, 1974): 37. Kovtun notes that Malevich writes about "Februaryist" painting and poetry, and that "judging from the context, this definition was close to the concept of *zaum* realism." The letter is not mentioned in Kovtun's later publication of a selection of Malevich's letters from the Pushkin House Archives, Leningrad, in *Ezhegodnik rukopisnogo otdela Pushkinskogo doma na 1974 god* (L, 1976).

4. 27 May 1915 (dated by postmark). K.S. Malevich, "Pis'ma k M.V. Matiushinu," publikatsiia E.F. Kovtuna in *Ezhegodnik rukopisnogo otdela Pushkinskogo doma na 1974 god* (L, 1976): 185-86.

5. May, 1915. Kovtun, *Ezhegodnik:* 178, 180.

6. 29 May 1915 (dated by postmark). Kovtun, *Ezhegodnik:* 186.

7. Kovtun, *Ezhegodnik:* 181.

8. 25 September 1915. Kovtun, *Ezhegodnik:* 180-81.

9. 24 and 28 September 1915 (dated by postmarks). Kovtun, *Ezhegodnik:* 187.

10. 22 November 1915, (dated by postmark). Kovtun, *Ezhegodnik:* 188.

11. 25 November 1915, (dated by postmark). Kovtun, *Ezhegodnik:* 189.

12. 19 October 1915, (dated by postmark). Kovtun, *Ezhegodnik:* 188.

13. Undated and incomplete letter to Matiushin, Archives of the Tretiakov Gallery, Moscow; f. 25, ed. 9, no. 20. An English translation of the entire portion of the letter may be found in K.S. Malevich, *The Artist, Infinity, Suprematism,* Troels Andersen, ed. (Copenhagen, 1978): 208-9. Andersen suggests the letter dates from May 1914, without giving a reason. In view of its subject, it would seem that late 1915, or even early 1916, would be a more likely date.

    Malevich mentions his early acquaintance with Nikolai Roslavets in his "Autobiography," edited and published by Nikolai Khardzhiev in *K istorii russkogo avangarda* (Stockholm, 1976): 116.

14. After the Revolution Malevich himself would produce three-dimensional "architectural models" based on Suprematist elements. The relationship of both Kliun's and Tatlin's "0-10" sculpture to the later Constructivist movement has yet to be explored.

15. M. Matiushin, "O vystavke 'poslednikh futuristov'," *Ocharovannyi strannik,* al'manakh vesennii (1916): 18.

16. In literature the work of writers such as Walt Whitman, D.H. Lawrence, James Joyce and Andrei Biely derived forms from occult concepts, as did the early abstract painting of Kupka, Mondrian, Kandinsky and Malevich.

17. For example, Daniel Robbins, *The Formation and Maturity of Albert Gleizes: A Biographical and Critical Study, 1881-1920,* unpublished Ph.D. dissertation (New York University, 1975); Margit Rowell and Mladek Meda, *František Kupka, A Retrospective;* exhibition catalogue, The Solomon R. Guggenheim Museum (NY, 1975); Rose-Carol Washton Long, *Kandinsky: The Development of an Abstract Style* (Oxford, forthcoming); Linda Dalrymple Henderson, *The Artist, "The Fourth Dimension" and Non-Euclidean Geometry 1900-1930: A Romance of Many Dimensions,* unpublished Ph.D. dissertation (Yale University, 1975).

18. Kulbin's pan-psychism is expressed most completely in "Svobodnoe iskusstvo, kak osnova zhizni," *Studiia impressionistov* (SP, 1910): 3-14. The summary of his esthetics given here is taken from this work and also from "Svobodnaia muzyka," *Studiia impressionistov* (SP, 1910): 15-26; "Garmonia, dissonans i tesnyia sochetaniia v iskusstve i zhizni," *Trudy vserossiiskogo s'ezda khudozhnikov v Petrograde.* Dekabr', 1911-Ianvar', 1912, I (P, 1914): 35-40; Statement (untitled) in catalogue *Salon 2* (Odessa, 1910-1911): 19. A discussion of Kulbin's esthetics and quotations from archival material are to be found in L.F. D'iakonitsyn, *Ideinye protivorechiia v estetike russkoi zhivopisi kontsa 19—nachala 20vv.* (Perm, 1966).

19. As we shall note below, Kulbin's notion of the painting as 'symbol' derived from the theory of equivalents of Helmholtz and its more recent elaborations by Wundt. In

order to avoid postulating a different physical mechanism for each kind of sense perception, Wundt maintained that it was possible that the variety of impressions received by the brain was due not to any material difference in the transmission of the stimulation, but rather to periodic phenomena involved in its impression on the brain. To Kulbin this may have seemed to indicate that the mental "sign" was equally a result of all the senses and thus if it were "projected" as a painting, the form would naturally be related to them all. Thus it was said that Kulbin even believed in painting odors, tastes, and so forth.

20. See the discussion following Bobrov's paper at the 1911 artists' congress: S.P. Bobrov, "Osnovy novoi russkoi zhivopisi," *Trudy khudozhnikov:* 44.

21. In "Svobodnaia muzyka": 24.

22. *Grundzüge der physiologischen Psychologie,* 1st ed., 1874; 6th ed., 1908-1911, 3v. Published in English as *Principles of Physiological Psychology* (London, NY, 1904).

23. *Elemente der Psychophysik* (Leipzig, 1860); Published in English as *Elements of Psychophysics* (NY, 1966). This is a translation of volume one only.

24. Republished in 1889. Interestingly, there was another edition published in 1907, the year before Kulbin's theories began to appear.

25. Of course the German psychologists themselves wrote widely about esthetics. Fechner was one of the first to attempt statistical studies in art, Helmholtz explained to painters what means should be used for successful illusion, and Theodor Lipps, best known for his theory of empathy, also made special studies of music and vision. In his *Psychologische Studien,* which appeared in 1905, he made extensive application of the work of Fechner, Helmholtz and Wundt to esthetics. It is notable that here, as Kulbin did in the case of color, Lipps stressed that musical consonance and dissonance are a result of tones mixing in the *soul,* rather than in the ear.

26. *Modern Chromatics, with Application to Art and Industry* (London, NY, 1879).

27. *Modern Chromatics:* 273. The italics are Rood's.

28. *Modern Chromatics:* 277. There is no reason to suppose that Rood is not somewhat indebted here to Fechner and Helmholtz.

29. In Berlin and Munich, between 1854 and 1858.

30. William Innes Homer, *Seurat and the Science of Painting* (Cambridge, Mass., 1964) contains a short biography of Rood and a careful estimation of his influence on the Neo-Impressionists.

31. *Die moderne Farbenlehre mit Hinweisung auf ihre Benutzungen in Malerei und Kunstgewerbe* (Leipzig, 1880); *Théorie scientifique des coleurs et leurs applications à l'art et à l'industrie* (Paris, 1881).

32. *Die Lehre von den Tonempfindungen als Physiologische Grundlage für der Theorie des Musik;* first published in 1863. Published in English as *On the Sensations of Tone as a Physiological Basis for the Theory of Music,* Alexander J. Ellis, trans. (London, 1885).

33. *On the Sensations of Tone* (1885): 330-31. The expressive power of "dissonance" was a concept Malevich often referred to; in the first decade of the twentieth century it played a central role in much of Russian and German modern music and art. Therefore it does not seem quite reasonable to suppose, as Andersen does, that Malevich was indebted only to Leger for the use of this term. See *K.S. Malevich, Essays on Art 1915-1933,* I, Troels Andersen, ed. (London, 1969): 10-11.

34. Helmholtz in his *Handbuch der physiologischen Optik* (Leipzig, 1867) had maintained that we perceive the world through a system of "signs." Sensory stimuli, he said, produce a 'sign' or 'token' or 'symbol' in the brain which is related to the stimulating object in some lawful and predictable way, but which need not resemble or 'equal' reality in any way, since it is the product entirely of the sense organ and the mind. In *Grundzüge der physiologischen Psychologie* (1874) Wilhelm Wundt also examined sensation as a symbol and tried to define its nature more precisely.

It will be noted that Kulbin's view of the nature of art has much in common with that of Maurice Denis. In his article "Definition du neo-traditionnisme" published in 1890, Denis asserts that the artist derives from nature a symbol, and that this is the expressive form. The work of art, he says, comes unconsciously from the soul, and the emotion is transmitted via line, form, and color, not the objects represented. It is futile to speculate on whether or not Kulbin had read this particular article, but probably sooner or later he knew Denis' theories. In any event, Denis' concept of the artistic process, as given in this and his later article, "De Gauguin et de Van Gogh au classicisme" (*L'Occident,* May 1909) seems also to rely heavily on Helmholtz's explanations of vision and esthetics.

A further elaboration of this idea is the use of the term "impression" for the symbol which is "impressed" on the brain. Thus the transference of this pattern to the canvas was sometimes called "impressionism."

35. M. Matiushin, "O knige Gleza i Metsanzhe 'Du Cubisme'," in the journal *Soiuz molodezhi,* 3 (March, 1913): 25-34. In this article Matiushin translated and paraphrased sections of *Du Cubisme* and printed them alternately on the page with selections drawn from P.D. Uspensky's *Tertium Organum.* Slightly later he edited and published another translation of *Du Cubisme* by his sister-in-law, E. Nizen. There was also a third translation, by Max Voloshin, published in Moscow by *Contemporary Problems.*

36. M. Matiushin, "O knige . . .": 25.

37. In his review of "Zero-Ten" Matiushin wrote: "The whole difficulty in the execution of his idea consists in the denial of form working to the detriment of color. Color should be so much higher than form that isn't pounded into any squares, angles, and so forth." "O vystavke 'poslednikh futuristov' ": 17.

38. Published in 1932, this book describes experiments carried on from 1923 at the Institute of Artistic Culture by Matiushin and his students.

39. Markov's discussion in this article, especially his use of "dissonance" and "free art" may be indebted to N. Kulbin, who used these terms in 1910. Markov may also have profited somewhat from Kandinsky whose paper, "On The Spiritual in Art," was read by Kulbin at the Second All Russian Congress of Artists in December 1911.

40. Markov, "Printsipy novago iskusstva" *Soiuz molodezhi,* II: 17.

41. Markov, ibid.: 16.

42. Malevich, "From Cubism and Futurism to Suprematism. The New Realism in Painting." (1916) in *Essays,* I: 19.

43. Malevich, *The Non-Objective World,* (NY, 1959): 68. This is an English translation made from the German Bauhaus Book, *Die gegenstandlose Welt.*

44. This discussion of Malevich's esthetic ideas is for the most part derived from his essays and his major theoretical work, *The Objectless World.* See K.S. Malevich *Essays on Art,* Troels Andersen, ed., I (London, 1968), II (London, 1969).

45. K. Malevich, *Ot kubizma i futurizma k suprematizmu* (M, 1916): 21.

46. K. Malevich, "An Attempt to Determine the Relation Between Color and Form in Painting," *Essays* II: 130.

47. *Ot kubizma . . .:* 21.

48. *Malevich,* Stedelijk Museum catalogue, Troels Andersen, ed. (Amsterdam, 1970): 122, 125.

49. Note that Malevich is here assuming the same kind of interaction of color and form as did Matiushin, but the operation has been placed by Malevich very specifically in the psychological realm.

50. Appendix: 109.

51. The Suprematists showed completely white canvases at an exhibition in 1923.

52. Malevich's front cover for N. Punin, *Pervy tsikl lektsii chitannykh na kratkosrochnykh kursakh dlia uchitelei risovaniia* (P, 1920).

53. K. Malewitsch, *Suprematismus die gegenstandlose Welt* (Cologne, 1962): 254.

54. There has been much speculation on the influence of Western art on Russian modernism, but none on the transmission of ideas in the other direction: from Russia further West. Certainly there was ample opportunity for the flow of information in this direction. Alexandre Mercereau was a direct link from Russia to Gleizes, Metzinger, Marinetti, and Leger. Members of the Russian art world were often in Paris, Munich, or Berlin. Western artists exhibited in Russia. It is a topic which should one day be explored.

55. For an exceptionally lucid and revealing discussion of the role of emotion and the interest in its transmission in modern European art, and the relation of this to the designa-

tion "Expressionism," see Donald E. Gordon, "On the Origin of the Word 'Expressionism'," in *Warburg and Courtauld Institute Journal,* v. 29 (1966): 368-85.

56. Anderson, *Malevich:* 116.

57. Malevich, *Essays,* I: 41.

Appendix

K. Malevich
From Cubism to Suprematism
The New Realism in Painting

Petrograd
1916

L. Ya. Ganzburg Pub., 11 Mytninskaia Street

From Cubism To Suprematism In Art,
To The New Realism Of Painting, To Absolute Creation

Space is a receptacle
without dimension into
which the intellect
puts its creation.
May I also put in my
creative form.

All former and contemporary painting before Suprematism, and sculpture, the word, and music were enslaved by the form of nature, and they await their liberation in order to speak in their own tongue and not depend upon the intellect, sense logic, philosophy, psychology, the various laws of causality and technical changes in life.

That was the time of Babel in art.

The art of painting, sculpture, the word, was up until now, a camel loaded with all kinds of rubbish of odalisques, with Egyptian and Persian kings, with Solomons, Salomes, princes, princesses and their favorite little dogs, with desire, and the fornication of Venuses.

Up until now there were no attempts at painting as such, without any attribute of real life.

Painting was a necktie on the starched shirt of a gentleman and a pink corset holding in the swollen stomach of a fat lady.

Painting was the esthetic side of a thing, but it never was original and an end in itself. Artists were legal investigators, police officials who composed various reports about spoiled produce, burglaries, murders and homeless tramps.

Artists were also lawyers, cheerful story-tellers, psychologists, botanists, zoologists, archeologists, and engineers, but there were no artist-creators.

Our Itinerants used to paint pots on fences in Little Russia and tried to convey the philosophy of weaklings.

The youth closer to us were occupied with pornography and turned painting into sensual, lascivious rubbish.

There was not the realism of painting as an end in itself, there was not creation. One cannot even count the idealization of Greek statues, there there was only the desire to improve a subjective "I."

Neither can one count pictures where there is exaggeration of real forms, but also copies of nature: icons, Giotto, Gauguin, etc.

Creation is present in pictures only where there is form which borrows nothing already created in nature, but arises out of the painted masses without repeating and without altering the primary forms of the objects of nature.

Futurism, having forbid the painting of female hams and the copying of portraits, removed perspective, too.

But even it introduced the prohibition not in the name of the emancipation of painting from those principles already mentioned—the Renaissance, antiquities, etc.—but because of the change in the technical side of existence.

The new iron, machine life, the roar of automobiles, flash of searchlights, growl of propellers, awakened the soul which was snoring as it suffocated in the cellar of its enumerated mistakes.

The dynamism of movement suggested the idea of promoting dynamism in the plastic art of painting also.

But the effort of Futurism to convey a pure painted plasticity as such was not crowned with success; it was not able to part with objectness in general, and only broke up the objects for the sake of achieving dynamism.

And the latter was achieved when the intellect was half expelled, the old corn of the habit of seeing objects as entities and tirelessly comparing them with nature.

But the fact that in the picture the construction of things going by is intended to transmit an impression of a state of motion in nature, moves the goal of achieving a pure painted plasticity in Futurism still further away.

Once such a task is set up, operation with real forms to obtain the impression is unavoidable.

But, nevertheless, Cubo-Futurism on its face, the breach of the integrity of objects, their breaking and truncation, hastens the annihilation of objectness in creative art.

The Cubo-Futurists assembled everything onto a square and broke them up, but didn't burn them up. Too bad!

They took painting out of the fashion shops, the dry goods and perfumers shops, and dressed it in our machine and ferro-concrete age.

The unusual strength of unreal objects, their rapid changing, surprised the Futurists, and they began to look for a means of transmitting the modern condition of life.

The very construction of a picture arose from finding points on the plane where the position of real things at their rupture or encounter would convey the time of greatest speed.

Locating these points may be accomplished at will, independent of the physical law of naturalness and perspective.

Therefore we see in Futurist pictures images of smoke, clouds, sky, horses, automobiles and various other objects in positions and places which do not correspond to nature.

And the condition of objects became more important than their essence and sense.

We saw an extremely unusual picture. The new order of objects forced the intellect to shudder and critics threw themselves like dogs from under a gate upon the artists.

Shame on them!

And enormous strength of will was needed to violate all the rules and to strip the coarsened skin from the soul of Academism and to spit in the face of common sense.

Good for them!

But while they are rejecting intellect and advancing intuition and the unconscious, at the same time Cubo-Futurists in their pictures are using forms created by the intellect for its own end.

Intuition could not express all the unconscious in the real aspect of particular forms.

In the art of the Futurists we see all the forms of real life, and if they are situated in inappropriate places, then this is done not subconsciously, but has its lawful, conscious justification in eliciting an impression of the chaos of movement in modern life.

Intuition was only able to find a new beauty in objects already created (Cubism).

Intellect, purpose, and consciousness are higher than intuition. They create a completely new form out of nothing, or perfect a primary form. From a two-wheeled cart to the locomotive, the automobile, the airplane.

While to the intuitive feeling is ascribed a higher ability to prophesy and to anticipate time.

A feeling that draws into real life the ever newer and newer from some unconscious void.

In art there is no proof of this. Intuition tried to find the new, the esthetic, only in already created things.

Intellectual creation is preceded by purpose and its means is self-consciousness.

But intuitive creation is unconscious and does not have purpose and an exact answer.

Futurist pictures do not vindicate that which the construction of the picture, the calculation of the order or the problem of the arrangement of things, tries to prove.

If we take any point in a picture we will find in it a retreating or approaching thing, or a contained colored space.

But we will not find the main thing, a painted form as such.

The element of painting here is nothing more than the outer clothing of the given thing.

And the size of the painting was given by how large a form was needed for its own purpose, and not vice-versa.

By advancing in pictures a painted plastic dynamism as something new, without abolishing objectness, the Futurist picture was reduced to 1/20 without losing its strength of motion.

It seems to me that it is necessary to convey purely colored motion in such a way that the picture cannot lose a single one of its colors. Motion, the running of a horse, a locomotive, can be conveyed by a monotoned pencil drawing, but not the motion of red, green, and blue masses.

Therefore one must turn directly to the painted masses as such, and look in them for the forms inherent to them.

In Futurism we meet mainly an appeal to objects and an operating with them, which must be given up for the sake of the pure creation in painting of new creative forms.

Dynamism in painting is only painted masses rioting toward an exit out of the thing to self-characteristic forms which do not mean anything, i.e., to the rule of purely self-sufficient painted forms over the intelligent, to Suprematism and to the new realism in painting.

I say: Futurism, via an Academism of forms, moves toward dynamism in painting.

Cubism, via the annihilation of the thing, moves toward pure painting.

And both efforts in essence aspire to a suprematism of painting, to triumph over the utilitarian forms of the creative intellect.

If one considers Cubism, the question arises, by what energy of the things is the intuitive feeling prompted to ecstasy and activity; We will see that the energy of the painting is secondary; a painting was not the esthetic side of a construction which emerged from the interrelationships of the colored masses.

The object itself, and also its essence and purpose, the sense or desire to present the object more fully (which many Cubists think), also were unnecessary trouble.

The intuitive feeling found new beauty in things—an energy of dissonances resulting from the meeting of two forms.

Things have in themselves a mass of moments of time. Their aspects are diverse and consequently the painting of them is also diverse. All these aspects of time in things and their anatomy—the layer of a tree, etc.—became more important than essence, and they were taken up by the intuition as the means for constructing a picture. Moreover, these means were designed so that the unexpectedness of the meeting of two anatomical structures would give a dissonance of the greatest tension, and this was used to justify the appearance of portions of real objects in places which do not correspond to nature.

Thus we were deprived of the idea of the whole thing by dissonances of things. With relief we can say there ceased to be two-humped camels laden with the rubbish mentioned above.

An object drawn according to the principle of Cubism may be considered finished when its dissonance is exhausted. All the repetitious portions may be omitted by the artist. But if the artist finds too little tension in the picture, then he is free to get it from another object.

In the principle of Cubism there is another very valuable task—not to convey objects, but to make a picture.

But the principle that every real form not created because the demands of the painting does it violence, is still not realized in Cubism.

If in previous centuries the artist sought the thing, its sense, essence, and tried to demonstrate its purpose, then in our era of Cubism the artist has destroyed the thing as such, and its sense, essence and purpose.

Things, objects in the real world, disappeared like smoke for the new standard of art.

And for a survey of objectness, like attributes in the Middle Ages, my eyes can be taken into a waxworks museum.

Cubism and Futurism created a picture from fragments and sections of objects through dissonances and motion. Intuition was crushed by the energy of objects and did not achieve a self-sufficiency of painting.

Cubo-Futurist pictures were created according to several principles:

1) artificial sculpture in painting (modelling of forms)
2) real sculpture (collage), relief and counter-relief
3) the word

In Cubism a painting was expressed mainly on the plane, before that it was a means of illumination!

As to the painted planes in Cubism, they were not ends in themselves, but rather their painted form served for dissonance. And the form itself was one which could give a strong dissonance when straight lines, curves, etc., were directed toward it.

Every painted plane which has been turned into a bulging painted relief is artificial sculpture, and every relief, projection, turned into a plane is painting.

And so in the art of painting the intuition did not create forms which emerged from the mass of painted material; there was not drawn out of a block of marble the cube, square, sphere, etc., inherent in it.

We encounter ecstasy of intuition as combinations in a picture. But intuition was also ecstatic with paintings of a pot on a fence, with a painted sunflower. . . .

Deformity of the human body and other forms depicted in pictures come from the fact that the creative will is not in agreement with these forms, and it carries on a struggle with the artist for its exit out of things.

The creative will up to now has been squeezed into the real forms of life. And deformity is the struggle of the creative power, out from the misery of confinement. This creative power, will, I call A.B. Abism in art, the safeguarding self-sufficiency of every art, whose forms will be a new revelation—of a painted realism of masses, of materials, of stone, iron and other things.

Thus, for example, the human form is not intrinsic in a block of marble. Michelangelo in sculpting David did violence to the marble, he mutilated a piece of good stone. It didn't become marble, it became David.

And he erred deeply if he said that he drew David out of the marble.

The ruined marble was defiled first by the thought of Michelangelo about David whom he squeezed into the stone and then set free like a splinter from a foreign body.

One must extract from marble those forms which could arise out from its own body, and a carved cube or other form is more valuable than any David.

The same in painting, the word, music.

The striving of the artistic powers to direct art along the path of intellect produced a zero of creativity. Even in the very strongest ones there are real forms: distortion.

Distortion was brought almost to the moment of vanishing by the strongest, but it didn't exceed the bounds of zero.

But I have transformed myself into a zero of form and gone beyond "0" to "1."

Believing that Cubo-Futurism has fulfilled its tasks, I am crossing over to Suprematism, to the new realism in painting, to objectless creation.

In time I will say more about Suprematism, painting, sculpture and the dynamics of musical masses.

June, 1915   K. Malevich

Illustrations

1
Kazimir Malevich: *Morning in the Village after Snowstorm*, 1912.
Oil on canvas, 31 3/4 x 31 7/8 in.
The Solomon R. Guggenheim Museum, New York.
Photo: Robert E. Mates.

2
Mikhail Larionov: *Glass*, 1912.
Oil on canvas, 41 x 38 1/4 in.
The Solomon R. Guggenheim Museum, New York.
Photo: Robert E. Mates.

3
Natalia Goncharova: *Cats,* 1913.
Oil on canvas, 33 1/4 x 33 in.
The Solomon R. Guggenheim Museum, New York.
Photo: Robert E. Mates.

4

Kazimir Malevich: *Englishman in Moscow*, 1913-14.
Oil on canvas, 34 1/2 x 22 1/2 in.
The Stedelijk Museum, Amsterdam.

5
Kazimir Malevich: *Woodcutter,* 1912.
Oil on canvas, 37 x 28 in.
The Stedelijk Museum, Amsterdam.

6
Kazimir Malevich: *Suprematist Composition,* ca. 1916.
Oil on canvas, 38 1/2 x 26 1/8 in.
The Museum of Modern Art, New York.

7

Mikhail Matiushin, Kazimir Malevich and Aleksei Kruchenykh in July, 1913.
Private collection, Leningrad.

8

Kazimir Malevich: Sketch for set of *Victory Over the Sun,*
Act I, scene 1 and Act II, scene 1.
State Theatrical Museum, Leningrad.

9

Kazimir Malevich: *Study Suprematis 52 System A4,* ca. 1918.
Pencil on paper, 27 x 19 1/4 in.
The Stedelijk Museum, Amsterdam.

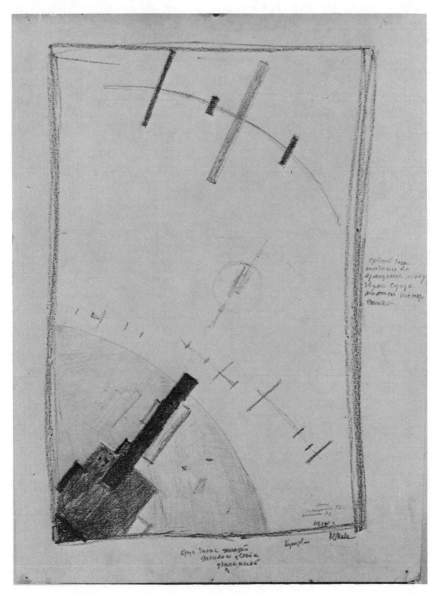

10
Kazimir Malevich: Illustration from *The Three (Troe)*, 1913.
4 x 5 in.

11
Kazimir Malevich: Installation "0-10. The Last Futurist Exhibition."
Petrograd, 1915.
Private collection, Leningrad.

12
Vladimir Tatlin: Installation "0-10. The Last Futurist Exhibition."
Petrograd, 1915.
Private collection, Leningrad.

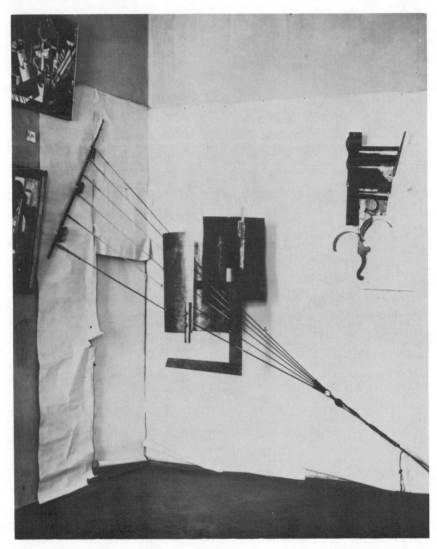

13
Kazimir Malevich: *Suprematist Compositions: Red Square and Black Square,* 1915.
Oil on canvas, 28 x 17 1/2 in.
The Museum of Modern Art, New York.

14
Kazimir Malevich: *Suprematist Composition,* ca. 1915.
Oil on canvas, 17 x 12 1/8 in.
The Alexander Dorner Trust, Busch Reisinger Museum, Harvard University.

Selected Bibliography

The bibliography has been selected for its relevance to the period and topic under consideration; few general historical works have been included. All but the most important reviews of exhibitions have been excluded. In many cases, only the best or most recent source for a particular piece of information has been listed.

Alloway, Lawrence. "Systemic Painting." *Minimal Art: A Critical Anthology,* ed. Gregory Battcock. New York, 1968, 37-60.
Alvard, Julien. "Les Idées de Malevich." *Art d'aujourd'hui,* 5 (July 1953), 16-21.
Andersen, Troels. *Malevich.* Catalogue raisonné of the Berlin Exhibition 1927. Amsterdam, 1970.
———. *Moderne Russisk Kunst 1910-1925.* Copenhagen, 1967.
———. *Vladimir Tatlin.* Catalogue: Moderna Museet. Stockholm, 1968.
Apollonio, Umbro, ed. *Futurist Manifestos.* New York, 1973.
Apollon. St. Petersburg, 1909-1917.
Baljeu, Joost. "The Problem of Reality with Suprematism, Constructivism, Proun, Neoplasticism, and Elementarism." *Lugano Review,* 1, 1 (1965), 105-24.
Barooshian, Vahan D. *Russian Cubo-Futurism 1910-1930.* The Hague, 1974.
Belloli, Carlo. *Russkii vklad v plasticheskie avangardy.* Milan, 1964.
Bergson, H. *The Creative Mind,* trans. M.L. Andison. New York, 1945.
———. *Intellektual'noe usilie: zametka o psikhologicheskom proiskhozdenii rashei very v zakon prichinosti.* St. Petersburg, 1913.
———. *Introduction to Metaphysics,* trans. T. E. Hulme. New York, 1912.
———. *Materiia i pamiat'.* St. Petersburg, 1911.
———. *Psikhofiziologicheskii paralogizm i snovideniia.* St. Petersburg, 1913.
———. *Sobranie sochinenii,* 5 vols. St. Petersburg, 1913-1914.
Bergson, H. *Tvorcheskaia evoliutsiia.* Moscow, 1909.
———. *Vospominanie nastoiashchago.* St. Petersburg, 1913.
———. *Vospriiatie izmenchivosti.* St. Petersburg, 1912.
———. *Vremia i svoboda voli,* s prilozheniem statei "Vvedenie k metafiziku." Moscow, 1911.
Berninger, H. and J. Cartier. *Pougny.* Tübingen, 1972.
Bialik, B.A. ed. *Russkaia Literatura kontsa XIX-nachala XX v. 1901-1907.* Moscow, 1971; *1908-1917.* Moscow, 1972.
Bibliografiia periodicheskikh izdanii Rossii, 1901-1916. 3 vols. Leningrad, 1958-1960.
Bobrov, S. "Osnovy novoi russkoi zhivopisi." *Trudy vserossiiskogo s'ezda khudozhnikov v Petrograde. Dekabr', 1911-Ianvar', 1912,* I. Petrograd, 1914, 41-43.
Boccioni, Umberto. *Gli scritti editi e inediti,* ed. Zeno Birolli. Milan, 1971.
Bowlt, John E., ed. *Russian Art of the Avant Garde: Theory and Criticism.* New York, 1976.
Brik, O. "Iz vospominanii." *Al'manakh s Maiakovskim,* eds. N. Aseev, O. Brik, S. Kirsanov. Moscow, 1934.

Burliuk, David. "Kubizm." *Poshchechina obshchestvennomu vkusu.* Moscow, 1913, 95-101.
———. "Nasha pervaia zima v Petere." *Color and Rhyme,* 55. Hampton Bays, New York, (1965), 25-28.
———. "Our Friendship with W.W. Kandinsky." *Color and Rhyme,* 51/52. Hampton Bays, New York, (1962/63), 9.
Calvesi, Maurizio. "Il futurismo russo." *Arte Moderna,* V, 44. Milan, 1967, 281-316.
Cachin, Françoise. "Futurism in Paris 1909-1913." *Art in America,* 62, 2 (March/April, 1974), 39-44.
Chalupecky, Jindrich. "Moscow Diary." *Studio International,* 185, 952 (February, 1973), 81-96.
Chamot, Mary. "The Early Work of Goncharova and Larionov." *The Burlington Magazine,* 97 (1955), 170-174.
Davis, Ivor. "Western European Art Forms Influenced by Nietzsche and Bergson before 1914. Particularly Italian Futurism and French Orphism." *Art International,* XIX, 3 (March 20, 1975), 49-55.
D'iakonitsyn, L.F. *Ideinye protivorechiia v estetike russkoi zhivopisi kontsa 19–nachala 20 vv.* Perm, 1966.
Douglas, Charlotte, John E. Bowlt eds. *Kazimir Malevich 1878-1935-1978.* Special issue, *Soviet Union/Union Sovietique* 5, 2 (1978).
Dreier, Katherine. *Burliuk,* Pts. I, II. New York, 1944.
Fechner, G. *Elemente der Psychophysik.* 2 vols. Leipzig, 1860 [1889, 1907].
———. *Elements of Psychophysics.* I. New York, 1966.
Fry, Edward. *Cubism.* New York, 1966.
Gleizes, A. and J. Metzinger, "Cubism," trans. R.L. Herbert. *Modern Artists on Art.* Englewood, 1964, 1-18.
———. *Du Cubisme,* trans. E. Nizen, ed. M. Matiushin. St. Petersburg, 1913.
———. *O kubizme,* trans. Max Voloshin. Moscow, 1913.
Gordon, Donald. *Modern Art Exhibitions 1900-1916,* I, II. Munich, 1974.
———. "On the Origin of the Word 'Expressionism'." *Warburg and Courtauld Institute Journal,* 29 (1966), 368-85.
Grabar', I.E. *Istoriia russkogo iskusstva,* X. I, Moscow, 1968; II, Moscow, 1969.
Gramoty i deklaratsii russkikh futuristov. St. Petersburg, 1914.
Gray, Camilla. *The Great Experiment: Russian Art 1863-1922.* New York, 1962.
Greenberg, Clement. *Post-Painterly Abstraction.* Los Angeles, 1964.
Guro, Elena. *Osennii son.* St. Petersburg, 1912.
———. "Pered vesnoi." *Schast'e* 3, (1906).
———. "Ranniaia vesna." *Sbornik molodykh pisatelei.* St. Petersburg, 1905.
———. *Sharmanka.* St. Petersburg, 1909. [1914].
Habasque, G. "Documents inédits sur les débuts du Suprematisme." *Aujourd'hui: Art et Archetecture,* 4 (1955), 14-16.
Helmholtz, Hermann. *Handbuch der physiologischen Optik.* Leipzig, 1867.
———. *Die Lehre von den Tonempfindungen als Physiologische Grundlage fur der Theorie des Musik.* Braunschweig, 1863.
———. *On the Sensations of Tone as a Physiological Basis for the Theory of Music,* trans. Alexander J. Ellis. London, 1885.
Henderson, Linda. *The Artist, 'The Fourth Dimension' and Non-Euclidean Geometry 1900-1930: A Romance of Many Dimensions.* Diss., Yale University, 1975.
Hinton, C.H. *Chetvertoe izmerenie i era novoi mysli.* Petrograd, 1915.
———. *The Fourth Dimension.* New York, 1904.
———. *A New Era of Thought.* London, 1888.
———. *Vospitanie voobrazheniia i chetvertoe izmerenie.* Intro. P.D. Uspenskii, Petrograd, 1915.
Homer, William Innes. *Seurat and the Science of Painting.* Cambridge, Mass., 1964.
Ivanov, Georgii. *Peterburgskie zimy.* New York, 1952.
Izdebskii, Vladimir. "Griadushchii gorod." *Salon 2.* Odessa, 1910, 11-12.

Jakobson, Roman. "De la Poesie à la Linguistique." *L'arc*, 60 (1975), 18-19.
Jensen, Kjeld Børnager. "Marinetti in Russia 1910, 1912, 1913, 1914?" *Scando-Slavica*, XV (1969), 21-26.
Judd, Donald. "Malevich: Independent Form, Color, Surface." *Art in America*, 62, 2 (March/April, 1974), 52-58.
Kamenskii, Vasilii. *Ego-moia biografiia velikogo futurista*. Moscow, 1918.
———. *Kak ia zhil i zhivu*. Tiflis, 1927.
———. *Put' entuziasta*. Moscow, 1931.
———. *Zhizn' s Maiakovskim*. Moscow, 1940.
Kandinskii, Vasilii. "Soderzhanie i forma." *Salon 2*. Odessa, 1910, 14-16.
———. "O dukhovnom v iskusstve (zhivopis')." *Trudy vserossiiskogo s'ezda khudozhnikov v Petrograde. Dekabr', 1911-Ianvar', 1912*, I. Petrograd, 1914, 47-76.
Karpenter, Edvard. *Liubov' i smert'*, trans. and intro. P.D. Uspenskii. Petrograd, 1915.
Katalog kartin vystavki "Venok" 1908 g. Saint Petersburg, 1908.
Katalog. Vystavka "Sovremennykh techenii v iskusstve". Saint Petersburg, 1908.
Katanian, V. *Maiakovskii; literaturnaia khronika*. Moscow, 1961.
Kazimir Malevich. Exhibition catalogue, Galerie Gmurzynska. Cologne, 1978.
Khardzhiev, Nikolai. "Iz materialov o Maiakovskom." *30 Dnei*, 7 (1939), 82-85.
———. "Maiakovskii i zhivopis'." *Maiakovskii; materialy i issledovaniia*, eds. V.O. Pertsov, M.I. Serebrianskii. Moscow, 1940, 337-400.
———. "Turne Kubo-futuristov 1913-1914." *Maiakovskii; materialy i issledovaniia*, eds. V.O. Pertsov, M.I. Serebrianskii. Moscow, 1940, 401-27.
———. "Maiakovskii i Elena Guro." *Poeticheskaia kul'tura Maiakovskogo*, eds. N. Khardzhiev, V. Trenin. Moscow, 1970, 193-95.
———. "Maiakovskii i zhivopis'." *Poeticheskaia kul'tura Maiakovskogo*, eds. N. Khardzhiev, V. Trenin. Moscow, 1970, 9-49, 307-16.
———. " 'Veselyi god' Maiakovskogo." *Vladimir Majakovskij: Memoirs and Essays*, eds. Bengt Jangfeldt, Nils Ake Nilsson. Stockholm, 1975, 108-51.
———, ed. *K istorii russkogo avangarda*. Stockholm, 1976.
Khlebnikov, Velimir. *Neizdannye proizvedeniia*, eds. N. Khardzhiev, T. Grits. Moscow, 1940.
———. *Sobranie proizvedenii Velimira Khlebnikova*, eds. Iu. Tynianov and N. Stepanov. 5 vols. Leningrad, 1933.
Khudakov, S. "Literatura khudozhestvennaia kritika, disputy i doklady." *Osliny khvost i mishen'*. Moscow, 1913, 125-53.
Khudozhniki narodov SSSR, biobibliograficheskii slovar'. I, Moscow, 1970; II, Moscow, 1972; III, Moscow, 1976.
Kovtun, Evgenii. "Die Entstehung des Suprematismus/The Beginning of Suprematism." *Von der Fläche zum Raum: Russland 1916-24/From Surface to Space: Russia 1916-24*. Cologne, 1974, 32-47.
Kozloff, Max. "Malevich as a Counterrevolutionary (East and West)." *Artforum*, XII, 5 (January, 1974), 30-39.
Kruchenykh, Aleksei and V. Khlebnikov. *Igra v adu*. Moscow, 1912.
———. *Starinnaia liubov*. Moscow, 1912.
——— and V. Khlebnikov. *Mirskontsa*. Moscow, 1912.
———. "Poshchechina obshchestvennomu vkusu." This manifesto was signed also by D. Burliuk, Maiakovskii, and Khlebnikov. *Poshchechina obshchestvennomu vkusu*. Moscow, 1912. Reprinted in Markov, *Manifesty*, 50-51.
———. *Poluzhivoi*. Moscow, 1913.
———. *Dve poemy. Pustynniki. Pustynnitsa*. Moscow, 1913.
———. *Pomada*. Moscow, 1913.
———. Manifesto (untitled). *Sadok Sudei II*. Saint Petersburg, 1913. Signed also by D. Burliuk, Guro, N. Burliuk, Maiakovskii, Nizen, Khlebnikov and Livshits. Reprinted in Markov, *Manifesty*, 51-53.
———. "Novye puti slova." *Troe*. St. Petersburg, 1913. Reprinted in Markov, *Manifesty*, 64-72.

———. "Pervyi vserossiiskii s'ezd baiachei budushchego." *Za 7 dnei,* 28/122. St. Petersburg, 1913, 605-6.
——— and V. Khlebnikov. *Slovo kak takovoe.* Moscow, 1913. Reprinted in Markov, *Manifesty,* 53-58.
———. *Deklaratsiia slova, kak takovogo.* St. Petersburg, 1913. Reprinted in Markov, *Manifesty,* 63-64.
———. *Pobeda nad solntsem: opera v 2 deimakh 6 kartinakh.* Muzyka M.V. Matiushina, dekoratsii Kaz. S. Malevicha, prolog Viktor [Velimir] Khlebnikova. St. Petersburg, 1914.
———. "Victory Over the Sun," trans. Ewa Bartos, Victoria Nes Kirby. *The Drama Review,* 15, 4 (Fall, 1971), 92-124.
———. "Pis'ma k M. V. Matiushinu," ed. B. N. Kapeliush. *Ezhegodnik rukopisnogo otdela Pushkinskogo doma na 1974 god.* Leningrad, 1976, 165-76.
———. *15 let russkogo futurizma.* Moscow, 1928.
Kulbin, Nikolai. *Chuvstvitel'nost. Ocherki po psikhometrii i klinicheskomu primeneniiu eia dannykh.* Saint Petersburg, 1907.
———. "Salon 1909." *Luch sveta,* 1 (January 15, 1909), 5.
———. *Chto est' slovo (II deklaratsiia slova kak takogo).* St. Petersburg, 1914. Reprinted in *Gramoty i deklaratsii russkikh futuristov.* St. Petersburg, 1914, n.p.
———. *Die freie Musik. Die Anwendung der neuen Theorie der Kunstlichen Schaffung zur Musik.* St. Petersburg, 1910.
———. "Garmoniia, dissonans i tesnyia sochetaniia v iskusstve i zhizni." *Trudy vserossiisko-go s'ezda khudozhnikov v Petrograde. Dekabr', 1911-Ianvar', 1912,* 1. Petrograd, 1914, 35-40.
———. "Kubizm." *Strelets,* ed. A. Belenson. 1. Petrograd, 1915, 197-216.
———. *La musique libre. Application a la musique de la nouvelle théorie de la creation artistique.* St. Petersburg, 1910.
———. "Novyi tsik slova." *Gramoty i deklaratsii russikikh futuristov.* St. Petersburg, 1914, n.p.
———. (Statement–untitled). *Salon 2.* Odessa, 1910, 19.
———. "Svobodnoe iskusstvo, kak osnova zhizni." *Studiia impressionistov,* ed. N. Kul'bin. St. Petersburg, 1910, 3-14.
———. *Svobodnaia muzyka. Muzykal'nyi sbornik,* ed. N. Kul'bin. St. Petersburg, 1911.
———. *Svobodnaia muzyka. Primenenie novoi teorii khudozhestvennago tvorchestva k muzyke.* St. Petersburg, 1909.
———. "Svobodnaia muzyka." *Studiia impressionistov,* ed. N. Kul'bin. St. Petersburg, 1910, 15-26.
Lamač, Miroslav. "Malevič a jeho okruh." *Výtvarné Uměni* 8/9 (1967), 373-83.
Lankheit, Klaus, ed. *The Blaue Reiter Almanac.* New York, 1974.
Lapshin, V.P. *Soiuz russkikh khudozhnikov.* Leningrad, 1974.
Lentulova, M.A. *Khudozhnik Aristarkh Lentulov.* Moscow, 1969.
Larionov, Mikhail. "Luchistaia zhivopis'." *Oslinyi khvost i mishen'.* Moscow, 1913, 83-124.
———. "Luchisty; budushchiki." *Oslinyi khvost i mishen'.* Moscow, 1913, 9-48.
——— and Ilia Zdanevich. "Pochemu my raskrashivaemsia. Manifest futuristov." *Argus* (December, 1913), 114-18.
Lipps, Theodor. *Psychologisch Studien.* Munich, 1905.
Livshits, Benedikt. *Gileia.* New York, 1931.
———. *Polutoraglazyi strelets.* Leningrad, 1933.
———. *The One and a Half-Eyed Archer,* trans. and ed. John E. Bowlt. Newtonville, Mass., 1977.
Loguine, Tatiana. *Goncharova et Larionov.* Paris, 1971.
Maiakovskii, Vladimir. *Polnoe sobranie sochinenii,* eds. V. Trenin, N. Khardzhiev. Moscow, 1935.
———. "Vladimir Maiakovskii, tragediia." *Sobranie sochinenii v 8 tomakh,* I. Moscow, 1968.
Makovskii, Sergei. " 'Novoe' iskusstvo i 'chetvertoe izmerenie'." *Apollon* 7 (1913), 53-60.

Malevich, Kazimir S. *Ot kubizma k suprematizmu. Novyi zhivopisnyi realizm.* Petrograd, 1916 [1915].
———. *From Cubism to Suprematism. The New Realism in Painting,* trans. Charlotte Douglas. See Appendix, this volume.
———. *Ot kubizma i futurizma k suprematizmu. Novyi zhivopisnyi realizm.* Petrograd, 1916.
———. *Essays in Art 1915-1923,* 2 vols. ed. Troels Andersen. London, 1969.
———. *The World as Non-Objectivity,* III, ed. Troels Andersen. Copenhagen, 1976.
———. *The Artist, Infinity, Suprematism,* IV. Copenhagen, 1978.
———. "Pis'ma k M.V. Matiushinu," ed. E.F. Kovtun. *Ezhegodnik rukopisnogo otdela Pushkinskogo doma na 1974 god.* Leningrad, 1976, 177-95.
———. Letter to P. Ettinger, ed. Szymon Bojko. *Von der Fläche zum Raum/From Surface to Space.* Cologne, 1974, 53-56.
———. *Die gegenstandslose Welt,* Bauhausbucher 11, trans. H. von Riesen. Munich, 1927.
———. *The Non-Objective World,* trans. H. Dearstyne. Chicago, 1959.
———. *Suprematismus–Die gegenstandslose Welt.* Cologne, 1962.
———. *De Cezanne au suprematisme,* trans. J. and V. Marcade, V. Schiltz. Lausanne, 1974.
Marcade, Valentine. *Le renouveau de l'art pictural russe 1863-1914.* Lausanne, 1971.
Marinetti, F.T. "The Birth of Russian Futurism Milan, Paris, Moscow, Saint Petersburg." *Marinetti's Writings,* ed. R.W. Flint. New York, 1971.
Markov, Vladimir [Matvejs Waldemar] "Printsipy novago iskusstva." *Soiuz molodezhi.* 1 (April 1912), 5-14; 2 (June, 1912), 5-18.
Markov, Vladimir, ed. *Manifesty i programmy russkikh futuristov.* Munich, 1967.
———. *Russian Futurism.* Berkeley, 1968.
Martin, Marianne. *Futurist Art and Theory, 1909-1915.* Oxford, 1968.
Matiushin, Mikhail. "O knige Metsanzhe-Gleza 'Du Cubisme'." *Soiuz molodezhi,* 3 (1913), 25-34.
———. "Futurizm v Peterburge." *Pervyi zhurnal russkikh futuristov,* 1/2 (1914), 153-57.
———. "O vystavke 'poslednikh futuristov'." *Ocharovannyi strannik,* 10 (1916), 16-18.
———. "Russkie kubo-futuristy." *K istorii russkogo avangarda,* ed. Nikolai Khardzhiev. Stockholm, 1975, 129-58.
———. "Opyt khudozhnika novoi mery." *K istorii russkogo avangarda,* ed. Nikolai Khardzhiev. Stockholm, 1975, 159-87.
———. "Sproba novogo vidchuttia prostoroni." *Novaia generatsiia,* 11 (1928), 311-22.
———. *Zakonomernost' izmeniaemosti tsvetochnykh sochetanii.* Moscow, 1932.
Meyer, Franz. *Marc Chagall: Life and Work.* New York, 1965?
Milashevskii, V. *Vchera i pozavchera. Vospominaniia khudozhnika.* Moscow, 1971.
Nusberg, Lev. "Statements by Kinetic Artists." *Studio International,* 173, 886 (February, 1967), 60.
Ogonek. St. Petersburg, 1900-1917.
Petrie, Brian. "Boccioni and Bergson." *The Burlington Magazine,* CXVI, 852 (March, 1974), 140-47.
Punin, N. "Impressionisticheskii period v tvorchestve M.F. Larionova." *Materialy po russkomu iskusstvu,* 1. Leningrad, 1928, 287-91.
Radin, E. *Futurizm i bezumie.* St. Petersburg, 1914.
Robbins, D. "From Symbolism to Cubism." *Art Journal,* 23, 2 (1963-1964), 111-16.
Robel, Leon, ed. *Manifestes futuristes russes.* Paris, 1971.
Roethel, Hans K. *The Blue Rider.* New York, 1971.
Rood, O. *Modern Chromatics, with Application to Art and Industry.* London, New York, 1879.
———. *Die moderne Farbenlehre mit Hinweisung auf ihre Benutzungen in Malerei und Kunstgewerbe.* Leipzig, 1880.
———. *Théorie scientifique des coleurs et leurs applications à l'art et à l'industrie.* Paris, 1881.
Rose, Barbara. "ABC Art." *Minimal Art: A Critical Anthology,* ed. Gregory Battcock. New York, 1968, 274-97.

Rozenfel'd, I. "Intuitivizm i futurizm." *Maski,* 6 (1913-1914), 17-26.
Russian Avant-Garde, 1908-1922. Catalogue: Leonard Hutton Galleries. New York, 1971.
Rylov, A. *Vospominaniia.* Leningrad, 1960.
Sadok sudei. St. Petersburg, 1910.
Salon. Katalog internatsional'noi vystavki kartin, skul'ptury, graviury i risunkov. 1909-1910. Odessa, 1909.
Salon 2. Odessa, 1910.
Sharp, Willoughby. "Luminism and Kineticism." *Minimal Art: A Critical Anthology,* ed. Gregory Battcock. New York, 1968, 317-58.
Shenberg, Arnol'd. "Paralleli v oktavakh i kvintakh." *Salon 2.* Odessa, 1910, 16-18.
Shershenevich, Vadim, trans. *Manifesty ital'ianskogo futurizma. Sobranie manifestov.* Moscow, 1914.
Shklovskii, V. *Khod konia;* sbornik statei. Moscow, 1923.
————. "Zaumnyi iazyk i poeziia." *Poetika.* Petrograd, 1919, 13-26.
Soiuz molodezhi. I, Saint Petersburg, 1912; II, Saint Petersburg, 1912; III, Saint Petersburg, 1913.
Stoletie voennago ministerstva 1802-1902, VIII. St. Petersburg; I, 1902; II, 1908; III, 1909; IV, 1911.
Sudeikin, S. *Kul'bin.* St. Petersburg, 1912.
Tasteven, Genrikh. *Futurizm; na puti k novomu simvolizmu.* Moscow, 1914.
————. "Impressionizm i novyia iskaniia." *Zolotoe Runo,* 7/9 (1908), XVII-XIX.
Tomashevskii, K. "Vladimir Maiakovskii." *Teatr.* 4 (1938), 137-50.
Treugol'nik. Katalog. St. Petersburg, 1910.
Troe. Saint Petersburg, 1913.
Uspenskii, P.D. *Chetvertoe izmerenie, opyt izsledovaniia oblasti neizmerimago.* St. Petersburg, 1909.
————. *Tertium organum, kliuch k zagadkam mira.* St. Petersburg, 1911.
Wundt, W. *Grundzüge der physiologischen Psychologie.* 3 vols. Leipzig, 1874 [1908-1911].
————. *Principles of Physiological Psychology.* London, New York, 1904.
Vergo, Peter. "A Note on the Chronology of Larionov's Early Work." *The Burlington Magazine,* CXIV, 832 (July, 1972), 476-79.
Zdanevich, Ilia [Eli Eganbyuri]. *Nataliia Goncharova, Mikhail Larionov.* Moscow, 1913.
Zhadova, L. "Teatr Maiakovskogo." *Dekorativnoe iskusstvo SSSR,* 6, 187 (1973), 39-43.
————. "Tsvetovaia sistema M. Matiushina." *Iskusstvo,* 8 (1974), 33-42.
Zheverzheev, L. "Vospominaniia." *Maiakovskomu,* eds. V. Azarov, S. Spasskii. Leningrad, 1940.
Zolotoe Runo. Moscow, 1906-1909.

Index